Truck of Fools

El furgón de los locos

Truck of Fools

Carlos Liscano

TRANSLATED BY ELIZABETH HAMPSTEN

VANDERBILT UNIVERSITY PRESS • NASHVILLE

© 2004 Vanderbilt University Press
All rights reserved
First edition 2004

Title page illustration: Carlos Liscano
Design: Dariel Mayer
Printed on acid-free paper
Manufactured in the United States of America

El furgón de los locos was originally published in Spanish in 2001
by Editorial Planeta S.A., Av. Rivera 2019, Montevideo, Uruguay.
ISBN 9974-643-12-0. Published by arrangement with Julie Popkin,
Literary Agent, 15340 Albright Street #204, Pacific Palisades, CA 90272.

Library of Congress Cataloging-in-Publication Data

Liscano, Carlos, 1949-
    [Furgón de los locos. English]
    Truck of fools / Carlos Liscano ; translated by Elizabeth
Hampsten.—1st ed.
        p. cm.
    Includes bibliographical references and index.
    ISBN 0-8265-1464-2 (cloth : alk. paper)
    1. Liscano, Carlos, 1949—-Imprisonment. 2. Authors, Uruguayan—
20th century—Biography. 3. Political prisoners—Uruguay Biography.
I. Title.

PQ8520.22.18Z46513 2004   863.'64—dc22

CONTENTS

TRANSLATOR'S NOTE

If history is what is written by "the winners," these, in Uruguay, have yet to recognize the recent past, or set about recording it. After thirteen years of civil-military dictatorship (1972–1985), the regime gave up, mainly because public coffers were empty. Their declared enemy—the "seditious"—had been trounced before the military marched through Parliament on June 26, 1973. Tupamaros, Communists, labor leaders and workers, teachers, artists, doctors, writers, anyone opposed to the Ready Security Measures, and many not manifestly so, by then were either in prison, dead, or out of the country. A "return to democracy" in 1985 brought an elected government, political prisoners released for time served, and an agreement not to investigate or prosecute the civil-military government's human rights abuses. No one involved in kidnapping, torture, kangaroo courts, long imprisonments (the Uruguayan dictatorship's distinguishing feature), or general State terror need divulge these events. The State had abrogated its power to bring the lawless to justice, meaning torturers and their victims might chance to cross paths in the streets of Uruguay's towns and cities. So far, the civil-military alliance has revealed no records, admitted to nothing more aberrant than that someone sometime perhaps got carried away ("*Se le fue la mano*"). Lips are sealed. Nothing happened. There is no history to write about.

Certainly there are those who disagree, convinced there *is* a recent past to account for, difficult though confronting it may be. "Winning" presumably inspires going public with the glow of achievement; loss begs for silence. Yet a winner/loser split does not describe post-dictatorship Uruguay. The ostensible winners are the ones now locked in silence, and the purported losers are those who are exercising ingenuity to report, denounce, remember, and not lose sight of what happened to them and to their country during more than a lost decade. To call their productions a "history" of the times is probably stretching expectations of scholarship, given the lack of access to official government records. What is left for reconstructing this past is individual witnessing, or, as termed in Uruguay and elsewhere, the writing of *testimonios*.

The word *testimonio* does not translate satisfactorily as "testimony" in English, where one speaks of giving testimony before a court of law, or to describe a religious experience. In the sense I want to use it here, *testimonio* is a literary form strongly charged with political connotations. The years I'd call the "classical" *testimonio* period, during and immediately after dictatorships in Latin America, produced works that were not focused on the author in an autobiographical or reportorial sense, but presented him or her as a member of a particular political group, speaking for that group and its ideology, assuming the consent of the group, and perhaps even justifying the self in regard to the group. (Some of these first *testimonios* were written as interviews with a sympathetic reporter, or in collaboration with another writer.) Next came *testimonios* as novels, where an author, frustrated by lack of access to public records and even by protagonists' reluctance to divulge information, turns uncorroborated evidence into fiction, claiming a probable truth. A third and later *testimonio* category approaches what looks to me closer to memoir and autobiography, includes more analysis and criticism than earlier examples, and is exemplified by Carlos Liscano's *Truck of Fools*.

Certain male writers of *testimonios* have maintained that their life as political activists necessarily was as separated as possible from private life. (You can make love and revolution, but not raise a family.) They may mention the birth of a child, but not comment on a relationship with the mother, or report that they received packages in prison, but not mention what went into gathering and bringing food, clothing, books and other goods to the prison, the efforts almost certainly of women. In Carlos Liscano's testimonial recollections, family are present, if sometimes by their absence, almost as ghosts—the birth of his sister, to his annoyance, when he is seven; the death of his mother; and later of his father by suicide; his grief and effort at reconciliation by locating his parents' urns in the cemetery. Liscano explores the strange but probably not uncommon mutual fascination with a torturer termed his *responsable*, and at a point of despair in torture, describes how he nearly tricked guards into shooting him. These are not moments of glory, they are not the stuff of hero-making.

What Carlos Liscano has achieved in *Truck of Fools*, I think, is a re-integration of himself as a person, as a son and brother in the family, and as a political citizen. Far from repenting, in a closing poem he writes: "So I think that had there been another possibility/ for me I would not have wanted it. / Because, and forgive me for saying so, I owe / to that dream the joy of having / known some of the best of men." He speaks at length about his body, its suffering in relation to his "self," and with modest pride says at the very end: "All I ever asked of my body in torture was that it allow me one day to look them [my parents] in the face with dignity." This integration, this ability or willingness to draw together various parts of a life into a single account, rather than insisting that one has nothing to do with another, creates a book all of a piece. And one of its more remarkable effects has already been, in Uruguay, to give direction to others wounded and afraid as to how to speak and write about the histories they have so far kept silent.

Paired with *Truck of Fools* is my translation of "A Life Without Object(s)," an essay by Carlos Liscano on the prisoner's experience. Here Liscano talks about the absolute aloneness of being in prison, a state where one is left only with one's body and the word. Neither can be relied on, but both must be relied on in order to live.

"A Life Without Object(s)" ["Una vida sin objecto(s)"] is also published in a collection of essays and stories, *The Language of Solitude* (*El lenguaje de la soledad*, Cal y Canto, Montevideo, Uruguay, October 2000). Liscano first presented the essay under the title "El lenguaje de la soledad" as a conference paper at El Colegio de México in March 1999; it was subsequently published in the Uruguayan newsweekly *Brecha* for July 22, 1999; in *Revista Fractal*, No. XI, Mexico 1999; and in *Revista Teatro al Sur*, No. 12, Buenos Aires, September 1999. A bibliography in *El lenguaje de la soledad* lists publications to date by Carlos Liscano, as well as reviews and criticisms of his work.

A Life Without Object(s)

In November 1972 a prison for political prisoners was inaugurated in Uruguay, a strange prison, a sort of kingdom of contrary logic, where the word was central, but by its absence and distortion. It was a place where words lost the meanings that are more or less accepted by habit and by dictionaries, and acquired other, unexpected ones, beginning with the name of the place: *Libertad* Prison, the source of this oxymoron being the proximity of the prison to the town of Libertad. The official name of this Uruguayan institution was Reclusive Military Establishment Number 1. There was also, logically enough, a Reclusive Military Establishment Number 2, where women were incarcerated.

The prison was odd because its abuse was barely visible, but silent, violent, and highly effective. Its "ultimate purpose," as explained by the military and its supporting civilians—of whom there were many, and of whom many are alive today and in high State administrative positions—was the prisoners' mental and physical breakdown. As they had not been killed at the time of arrest nor in the months of torture that followed, inmates' every movement, action, and thought were frozen, in order to reach the same ends by other means.

Along with this secondary objective to be carried out in the prisons, the civilian and military government intended to found in Uruguay a millennial rule based on military training, for which they invented a jargon made up of words and phrases like "process," "chronogram," "institutions with dignity," "enemies of the country," "the civic-military," "institutional laws," and a great many slogans. Radio, television, and newspapers all adopted this lifeless "official idiom" that strained relations among citizens. Added to that were an infinite variety of solemn patriotic events; thought was disparaged in all of its forms, and mediocrities rose to every educational and cultural level—men and women who had spent their lives gnawing resentments now at last reached heights that their own dim wits never would have made possible.

Libertad Prison fit into that military-civilian jargon. At the entrance of the cellblock was an enormous sign that Dante might have envied: "One comes here to obey," meaning that no one entered that Uruguayan-built earthly paradise voluntarily. Prisoners were to undergo the punishment they deserved, and the Uruguayan army was sacrificing itself to see to it that sentences were served. Pleasure and joy were excluded by definition.

Libertad Prison consisted of a building and a group of five sheds. The building, ten meters above the ground on ninety-six columns, was divided into five floors divided into two sectors divided into two wings. Sheds were divided into two sections each. No one in the building could communicate with anyone in the sheds. Each floor was isolated from the others. Each section within a floor was separated from other sections, each wing separate from the other. Counting floors, sheds, sections, and wings, a thousand prisoners were divided among some thirty units unconnected to one another.

All this is complicated and not worth trying to understand. Not even prisoners ever had an exact idea of the swollen organization that governed the movements of individuals and of objects, the process for bathing, for washing and hanging up laundry, for serving food, sending and receiving mail, visits from relatives and lawyers, permissions, prohibitions, all of life.

When, after years, a person thought he knew how things worked, he realized he had not gone beyond the most superficial elements, that in its depths the organization had yet more complexities, caverns, dark places inscrutable to the most expert administrator. And furthermore, if he managed to dig deeper yet, the person could see there were so many exceptions to established procedures that actually every instance was a separate case for which the organizational plan had tried to find logical solutions, none of which ever were able to be organized into a consistent system. Even so, everything in the prison gave the impression of having its reason.

The landscape was a wilderness of metal and bars, populated by soldiers, dogs, truncheons, and regulations. A prisoner could dedicate himself for years to inventing reality, to naming what did not exist so that it would begin to exist. It was necessary to invent situations where happiness and a smile might appear spontaneously. And they did appear, they always turned up, and no one could understand what those characters were laughing about.

Isolation and bureaucratic complication characterized

Libertad Prison—isolation from the world, from the rest of the country, and of prisoners from one another, down to individual isolation. The prison looked like an artificial satellite on top of its columns, immobile on the planet Earth, set apart from society and nature. Prison life had changed into molecules that never-rendered the image of a whole body.

Instead there were rules: prisoners must walk always with their hands behind their backs and be identified by a number on the gray uniform, and on shirts, sheets, football pants, the number by which they were known, called, punished. Prisoners had no head of hair. They were shaved once a week, or every three or four days, or once a day—lucky ones might be shaved morning and night of the same day.

What was not specifically authorized fell into the category of the forbidden, a category highly particularized in the realm of reading. The forbidden included all of history from the French Revolution on, physics, chemistry, electronics, social sciences, Victor Hugo, Borges, Proust, Jardiel Poncela, Benedetti, the Marx Brothers, and the Latin-American Bible. No one could guess what authors were prohibited because military logic goes by margins too ineffable for the understanding of civilians, unless they be civilian members of The Process.

In that small jungle of compartmentalized spaces, rules, orders, contradictory statements, general and detailed arbitrariness, permanent and circumstantial arbitrariness—decided on by the highest thinking little heads of the military forces, and decided on also by the soldier of the moment—reality turned abstract. When the world is broken up and absurd, one becomes unglued, evolves into something else, something that at first one does not know what it is, and after a long while manages to organize in his head, or does not manage to and becomes lost in delirium and sorry madness.

A certain minor problem I understood only long after I had entered prison, at the time when I began to write: in prison there are no common objects, the sort used everyday on the outside. There is no clock, no chair, no cooking pot. You don't turn a light on and off, have no key to open or lock doors, there is no bathroom, or the bathroom is also the bedroom and dining room without a door, there is no necktie, no trousers, comb. One neither lights nor puts out a fire, has no money, does not buy, pay for things, make telephone calls, read the newspaper, turn on the radio or television. You end up forgetting what many objects are for and when to use them. This increases estrangement from the word. Utterances one knows lose their usefulness, pass to the category of things that live only in language, like the number pi.

The Obsession with the Word

The most forbidden object in prison was the word. If you spend a lot of time not speaking you get out of the habit. Given a human being's pig-headedness, which a prisoner shares by definition or he wouldn't be there, having broken some rule—not being able to speak makes speaking his only desire. The word takes on a value it did not have in normal life: being able to say something and be listened to and responded to becomes a marvel, the greatest of human marvels. That is when one discovers what he always knew but never had to state: that whatever one is, that sense of being comes from the word. He who cannot express himself or has no time to think of what or how to speak, does he exist?

Lack of opportunity for communication at first makes one obsessed with breaking isolation, determined to invent signals, make up tapping languages, sign languages. These strategies put an extraordinary value on speech. Speech thus becomes scarce, clear, and brief. No one has the luxury of long empty talk, or of choosing what seems merely objective when the word is so watched over and forbidden. So language gains in precision and loses in elaboration, a limitation I shall try to explain with a personal example.

This is what I experienced when I got out of prison: for years I had not spoken to more than one person at a time, because more than two were not allowed together in the prison yard or patio. Afterwards, with family and friends, eight or ten of us would be sitting around a table. Everyone would talk at once. According to my habits, I assumed that what others were saying had to be important; otherwise why would they be talking? So I wanted to hear them all, and would be in despair because all were talking at once. Then I realized that whatever any one person said was not being listened to; they'd interrupt each other, change the subject without the speaker seeming to care very much. It seemed impossible that this was conversation. Then it occurred to me they were not saying anything, they were just playing. People get together not to tell each other important things but to play with words. In the old prison days, whenever I was allowed to talk with someone on the patio, I'd talk for thirty or forty-five or sixty minutes (recreation time increased over the years), and say what I had to say. The other person would listen in silence, neither agreeing nor disagreeing. Two or three or four weeks later he'd answer, in thirty or forty-five or sixty minutes, everything my monologue had made him think about. It was like communicating by telegraph, one at a time.

The Speaking Animal

In that spot separated from the world that was *Libertad* Prison, there was another place even more isolated, and defined by its name, "The Island." The Island was where prisoners were placed who broke regulations or refused to obey orders, or rebelled against arbitrariness, or made mistakes, or had gotten into trouble with some military person. There was no shortage of causes for being sent to The Island.

The Island consisted of solitude, silence, and repression. You could not speak, ever. There was no light; drinking water was rationed, which, for reasons incomprehensible to a prisoner, might be given out at ten in the morning, six in the evening, or at three in the middle of the night. The *calabozo* (solitary cell) measured two meters by two meters of gray cement, separated from the actual door by a grill, and with a hole in one corner. Water ran along the walls and on the floor, wind blew through a crack at ceiling level. Twice a day the door opened and the prisoner was handed an aluminum plate of scalding hot food. Five minutes later it was taken away. No baths, no shaving, no seeing other faces. Hair cut once a week. A beard might grow for a month, but not a head of hair.

Sentence time is not measured in societal time: it is the time that remains in the sentence. For the recluse, the time remaining to the sentence begins the day confinement in the *calabozo* ends. The present is not the time of history, of work, of creation, of the struggle with other men and with things: it is a parenthesis apart from the world. The person being punished returns to the primordial solitude in which we were born. He turns into a full-time thinker because thinking is all there is to do. He is alone with his thoughts; awake sixteen hours a day, pacing the two and a half meters on the diagonal.

When a human being is alone, absolutely alone, without nature or culture or sun or artificial light, or sound, he is not in the world. So what's left? His body is what he is left with, and the word is what he thinks about. The word is the past, tradition, and culture. The body and the word make up the entire life of the person who is absolutely alone. But in that place the word is useless for naming what he does not have, or for communication. There is nothing, it is emptiness: water is not water, it is humidity on the walls. Sound is the squeak of a door. Light is what the eye invents in the dark, and the pictures he creates from stains on the walls. Odors are those of an animal and its dung. There is the body and there is the word, but the body is good neither for work nor for pleasure, and the word is useless for naming the absence of things, of people, lover, friends, neighbors, parents, children.

In that place, when skin began dropping off for lack of sun, all that mattered was oneself. One repeated to oneself: "I must stay alive, I must stay alive, in spite of everything. If the world collapses, I shall go on living." Although one did not quite know why, living seemed necessary. To survive, one concentrates so much on nature that one becomes only the body, one turns into a beast.

The word is the prisoner's only ally and also his worst enemy. For a beast it's enough to eat, drink, and sleep a few hours. Yet the word never stops menacing the poor beast. The word calls up remembrance, hope, unanswered questions, what he did not do and should have done. Within the word resides the human being. But one doubts he is still human, and doubts all the more when it occurs to the jailer, just for fun, to omit a prisoner's meal. In The Island there are no voices other than one's own for responses, stimulation, dissent, to remind one that it is better to be human than animal. One intuits that, without the word, animal is all that's left, and is convinced that the animal would survive better than oneself, who is cursed for being a speaking animal.

But now at the outer limit, the crushed and stained word invents a soft little voice that speaks, that invents the world again, in color, in sound, in agreeable odors, and in friendly familiar voices. Then the word becomes salvation again, it recreates itself all over—the birds whose names you never knew, a sunset in childhood, trees and their shade, a trivial little tune, the Pythagorean school rule about irrational numbers, a story by Dino Buzzatti about a king, and a goal you saw a favorite player make. Everything is alive again and in existence thanks to the power of one who, having nothing, discovers again that he possesses the word, which is what creates everything.

In this struggle the only objective is survival. The world has disappeared, one has oneself and is obliged to live with that individual. You can run yourself down, feel sorry for yourself, hate yourself a little, but you cannot declare total war or condemn the other, the one you are. Eventually you have to forgive yourself, believe in yourself; know that even being what it is, life is worth living.

One makes peace, respects his shortcomings, rescues something positive, illusory though it may be. Often is surprised to be talking alone. The first time, the surprise of hearing one's own voice can bring fear that talking to oneself is proof of having gone over the edge. Then you realize that speaking, although alone, is necessary and healthy. After that, reconciled, you tell yourself things, remember out loud, sing songs, form phrases you don't want to lose in the rush of thought.

From the Word to Freedom

When nothing is possible, one does what he can within the narrow bounds that remain, and, although it might not seem so, within those limits there is an almost limitless space. By a curious reversal, when a prisoner thinks of the world outside prison and compares it with his own, he feels he can exercise freedom better than can outsiders.

As he can do nothing to change things, a prisoner works on himself, which is the one material he is able to control. He dedicates twenty-four hours of the day to this transformation, one that forces him to change language in several stages, in various guises: who he is, the idea of himself, his self-representation before the guards, his relationship to the prisoner in the next cell, his secret past.

The lie that the prisoner constantly presents to the guard is watched by the persona he senses he really is. He lives representing and re-presenting himself constantly in a never-ending theatrical production. He can pretend to be the one who knows nothing, who does not understand, is distracted, stupid, crazy. Each of these representations demands consistency in action and word. The prisoner writes his part and plays it, he is his own theatrical work, and that work, in which his life is passing, implies one moral theme for the repressor and another for him. Even insanity has its consistent logic. The prisoner acts the madman in order not to go mad. Each step toward premeditated madness is an experiment in language. Which of the two am I: the madman or the one pretending to be mad?

Everything counts when facing the repressor, but one should not forget the second moral theme that is daughter to and dependent on the other: the theme of dignity. The prisoner is a defeated being, but his mere existence challenges the winners. In a prison for political prisoners, the prisoner always counts as "an enemy of society." To be an enemy of society sounds dramatic but turns out to be ridiculous. Mere existence now is resistance, and gives the weakest a power that the vanquisher does not have. For the vanquished, existence is enough to give the world significance. For the vanquisher, not even the death of the vanquished suffices; he watches the prisoner day after day, for months, years; sees that he keeps on existing, breathes, thinks, does things in silence. The vanquisher knows that what he sees is only an act. But as the prisoner has many costumes, the repressor never knows when he is facing an act and when he is before the real thing. The prisoner, to the guard, is a mystery. He will never know who the prisoner is, which makes the prisoner a powerful being, and free.

In the prison's disarticulated world, broken up, disconnected from the big world and at the same time divided into unconnected pieces, the world at first retreats. Over the years, little by little, prison begins to be reflected in language. Language organizes reality, gives it shape, imposes meaning, and thus modifies reality. In that manner, words return to their place, they return to conquer fragments of liberty. Now they have the advantage of the load taken on after the trip to the outer edges, there where the animal resides, and where the human being becomes confused with it.

One never gets over missing the real world, the world of the free. But it is reachable by an oblique line of irony and black humor. When nothing can get worse, there is nothing to laugh about. But later, as no one is more grotesque than a prisoner, everything can be the object of laughter. This gives extraordinary strength; one becomes the object of his own jokes, and that way saves himself. Language saves him again. The prisoner has gained control over the fear of death, has argued with it. He has not beaten death, but keeps him in sight. At a later date the prisoner can joke about his own situation. So why not do so with the situation of others, of the free, those who are outside, who do not know what true liberty is?

Reflecting on language, reaching the border where the human being begins to be only animal, can lead to disbelief in language. The word is culture, and culture, as the property of the vanquishers, is a lie, is repression, arbitrariness, abuse; it is the civil-military, the social sewage in the seat of power. Words become inane, all words, those of others equally with one's own. The prisoner distrusts language, himself, everything said, and thinks even scientific knowledge is an empty construction. All of which is healthy, because it develops the ability never to take oneself too seriously. But it is dangerous too, because it can lead to a total disbelief in the human being, which is the word.

Fortunately one comes to discover the essential words, those of friendship, of solidarity, the ones that name the tastes of bread and salt. And so little by little you again rescue the word, and a little timorously, very carefully, begin to remove it from the garbage where the dictatorship has buried it. You remember what you already suspected, or what you reach for as new knowledge: a human being is neither only a shining creature nor only a beast. A human being is both, and language reflects the two. That the torturer also has command of the word does not cancel out the value of the tortured person's silence, he who in torment swallows his answers. In spite of hypocrisy, lies, and the corruption of thought and feeling that every dictatorship wants to impose on life, there are words that are very important, and those should be saved so they can save us.

Solitude and solidarity, death and liberty, at one time or another have been objects of reflection for every prisoner, no matter the degree or the extent of his elaboration and development. I'll say briefly and modestly: in prison I became an adult, in prison my hair turned gray, in prison I made my best friends, in prison I became a writer. After fourteen years I feel that something of that journey to the limits of language is at the bottom of all I have written, in and after prison.

Truck of Fools

El furgón de los locos

For days, I've been in an army barrack, hooded to the shoulders; pants, T-shirt, undershorts, shoes all soaking wet. I am twenty-three years old. I don't know what day or what time it is. I know it is late at night. They have just brought me from the room where they torture; that's on the floor below, down the stairs to the left. You can hear screams, one person tortured, then another and another, all night. I don't think about anything. Or I think about my body. I don't think it; I feel my body. It's dirty, beaten up, tired, smelly, sleepy, and hungry. Just now, the world consists of my body and me. I don't say it to myself like that, but I know there is no one else but the two of us. It will be many years, almost thirty, before I can tell myself what it is I feel. Not tell myself "what I feel," but what it and I felt.

Two Urns in One Car

1

I have just turned seven. I am learning to tell time, but
don't have a clock. In those days only grownups have
clocks. A clock is a serious instrument, expensive,
needs to be taken care of, not for children.

The three of us live in an attic, my father, my mother,
and I. The attic, which one day will be my room, where
I'll live alone for almost ten years, is about twelve meters
square. The Liscano family lives there; that is, my family.
I barely know it yet, but I am a Liscano, a rare surname
in my country. I have learned to explain that I am not
Lescano, nor Lascano, nor Lezcano. Liscano, with an *i* and
with an *s*. A lifetime of explanations.

That night my father wakes me up. This never
happens. Why is he waking me, what does he want?

It's cold. I see my mother, dressed, sitting on the bed,
with a hand on her belly, trying to calm my father. Two
things I don't understand: my father waking me up for no
reason, and my mother, sitting there on the bed holding
onto her belly.

My father says we have to go to the hospital because
my little brother is to be born. Some months ago, two or
three or four, my mother said, as if by the way, that I was

to have a little brother. She was folding clothes to put away, and asked, "Would you like a little brother?"

Of course not. I was fine as I was.

But I could see my mother was not interested in my opinions. She was only informing me.

Now they have woken me up and I don't know what time it is. I don't know the time, not this specific time nor time in general. My father tries to dress me. My father is awkward, always is, no matter what he is doing. He is strong and awkward. My mother is much better than my father, always looks after me, is always gentle. My mother is strong and clever and gentle. So, although she barely moves, my mother helps my father dress me.

Between the two they get me dressed and we go out to the street, where it is night and colder than in the attic. A taxi comes by and we get in, a thirty-one-year-old man, a pregnant woman of twenty-five, a child of seven, and a bag. I know that at that moment that's how I think of it, the ages and details—that's the sort of child I am, a child who his whole life can't help counting and calculating everything set before him.

2

My mother, holding onto her belly, my nervous father, the bag of clothing, and I arrive at a hospital. I, a child, know exactly where I was born, in which hospital, what day, what year, what hour. And so I know this is not my hospital, the only one I've been in, where I was born. This one is luxurious, not like mine, a hospital for the poor.

Why is my little brother going to be born here, when I wasn't? I don't know, don't ask. One day my mother will explain. A textile worker like herself has a right to this hospital. When I was born she was a servant and did not have as many rights.

My father, who never understands much, leaves me in the waiting room. I don't know if he thinks I am a man, and that a man always looks after himself. Maybe he is so nervous he does not realize I am seven years old. But he leaves me there, and disappears with my mother.

I am left alone for hours. I have no one to talk to, nothing to eat or drink or play with. Here I am, a man of seven, solid as my father wishes me to be. Actually my father is of little importance to me. I try not to cause problems for my mother. I do what I have to do and come right back. She always knows everything, not my father. I sit down to wait for her. When she finishes she will return and tell me what she did. She always tells me everything. Not my father, who never has time, has no words. He does not talk, she explains everything. That's how they are.

I am in the waiting room of this hospital where there is nothing, and my little brother is going to be born. Here, where he will be born, there is not much of anything. There is a plant, a couple of chairs, a few people going by, and me. That is, I am truly alone.

The only more or less interesting object here is the clock on the wall. Nothing else of any use. I start staring at it and trying to guess what time it is. They've explained to me a little about telling time, but I still have not learned. I concentrate on trying to see what the clock does. So time passes. Once in a while I look. Suddenly I understand the logic of the hands. Every five minutes I look again. I realize now I know what time it is. But the clock does not advance as fast as I'd like in order to prove it to myself. If I have just seen that it's 2:20, it does not help much to tell me in five minutes that it is 2:25. I'd like the minutes to advance more quickly to test out my discoveries.

For long periods I forget about my father, who said he'd be back and has not shown up even once, about my mother who is in some floor above, about my little brother with whom I shall be able to play football. I have learned to tell time, that's what I have to tell my mother and father when I see them again.

3

Suddenly my father appears. He arrives tired and happy. It is almost seven o'clock in the morning. He tells me my mother and little sister are fine.

What's that? They promised me a little brother, not a little sister.

Well, it didn't turn out that way. It's a girl. A beauty.

For me this is inexplicable, illogical. I can't get it into my head that they would have made such a mistake. With a girl you can't play football or do anything. What do I do with a girl?

With the thought of the impossibility of a girl, I go home with my father in a taxi.

In the afternoon my grandmother takes me to see my

mother. She is in bed. Next to her is a crib with a bundle. This is "the girl" they got me, "the beauty."

It is May 24, 1956. Today I learned to tell time. Today my sister was born. Two things to last a lifetime.

4

Montevideo, May 27, 1972. Three days ago my sister turned sixteen, and tonight there is a party. When it begins, I don't show up. I know my mother will be worried. My father will suppose I'm wandering about, up to goodness knows what. My sister will think I'm not interested in her.

I had planned to go to the party, and said I would, but won't, can't. At two in the morning the military comes to get me at my house. They get me out of bed, barefoot and in an undershirt, put a hood on my head, tie my hands behind my back, and set me out on the sidewalk, facing the wall. Then they throw me into a pickup and off we go.

5

Libertad Prison, May 31, 1976. I've been a prisoner for four years. Just now my cellmate is Cholo González, a cane worker. Cholo was in prison before, and escaped from *Punta Carretas* prison in 1971. In 1972 he sought refuge in Chile. Then he went to Cuba. In 1975 he left Cuba by way of Moscow and Buenos Aires. His goal was Montevideo. When he got to Montevideo they arrested him, shot him in the face. After torture, they brought him to the prison and put him in my cell. Cholo is a labor union leader. He's had few years of schooling, but is a cultured, amiable, and loyal man.

The prisoners are desperate and passionate about making use of time. You must do something positive, something for life, not stand still, not be beaten down by the grilling. Soon after becoming acquainted, Cholo and I agreed that I'd help him study the Spanish language. He is certainly capable of holding his own in tough, complex debates in a large meeting, of organizing and leading people, traveling halfway around the world with false documents, but he has a hard time writing. With great modesty he accepts my offer to help.

I begin looking for a Spanish language book, and someone gives me a first-year high school text.

6

As I don't know how to start the course, I read the first lesson out loud and then comment on it, how to recognize a verb, a noun, an adjective. He points to a word he does not know, I try to explain what it means.

Then we go to the exercises for that lesson, we do them, and agree that every morning he will read the text, do the exercises, and in the afternoon I will correct them. Now he has his homework for the next day.

Little by little we gather dictations and writings. As he can't think of anything to write about, and thinks he has nothing to say, I ask him to write about things connected to his life and his work. So he tells me, in writing, how sugar cane is cut in Uruguay and how it is cut in Cuba, different techniques; how to make a sod house; how to make a thatched roof.

These are things I don't know and so, after correcting, I ask for more explanations, details. I learn, he learns, we complement one another.

I use a red pencil to correct Cholo's writings. Some time later he tells me it makes him angry to look at his notebook, so tidy, so perfect, with those marks I make. Each mark means besides that he has to write the word ten times to remember it, as I was taught in school. He does not like my method, but as we are serious and have agreed, he does it.

I think there is something that helps us understand each other: stories I've told him of my family, my parents who grew up in the country. In some way he and I are of the same mix, we came from nothing. Nothing in my country is not having a surname, an uncle, or a few friends whom everybody knows, having no connection to power. We come from nowhere and expect to be treated with respect. Why should we be respected? Well, for something, for something we are able to do. Stand up, for example. Study Spanish language in prison, for example.

7

One afternoon, after eating and before the Spanish lesson, the cell door opens and I am told I have a visitor. This is suspicious. It is Monday, I had a visit the Thursday before, today is not my turn. Nor is it the day for lawyers' visits, besides which I don't have a lawyer, because the one I had is also in prison, on the fourth floor. The Supreme Military Tribunal has named a representative to me, a colonel who acts as defender of several hundred prisoners. This gentleman never comes to see a prisoner in his cell. So it can't be a visit from either family or a lawyer.

The military uses this business of saying one has a visitor when they want to take a prisoner out of his cell to torture him. It does not matter if it's been years since his arrest, if they think it necessary they take him to a barrack to interrogate him again.

On the last visit, I saw my mother. As we barely have thirty minutes, it isn't worth my father's traveling fifty kilometers to see me for such a short time. My mother almost always comes alone. A coincidence: the last visit was May 27; I've been in prison exactly four years.

I leave the cell very suspicious. A couple of soldiers take me to the visitor's room. Empty cement benches, telephones in place next to the windows that separate the prisoner from the visitor.

After a few minutes, my father comes in. It's enough to look at him to know what happened. His eyes are red. He tells me my mother died. He adds that actually he should have been the one to die, because without her he does not care to go on living.

8

I don't know what to say to him, don't know where to hide. My mother has died at age forty-five. She will always, always, be forty-five years old. A time will come when I will have lived longer than she, will be older that she. Now she will be buried and I won't be there, won't be able to accompany my father, won't see my sister who will come from Buenos Aires for the burial. I can't, I can't do anything. It's all so big it does not fit into my head. Questions are so many and so large I don't know how to begin answering them.

In five minutes they have me say goodbye to my father; we embrace.

They take me back to the cell and I tell Cholo the little I know of what happened.

Right off, I don't know how, I make a plan: nothing has happened here. The military of course knows my mother died. If I show that it pains me, if I show I feel weak, they will jump at the chance to destroy me. Therefore, all must go on as usual.

I tell Cholo we have to continue the day's lesson. He says he'd rather not, that we can take the day off. I insist the lesson must go on, because that is the agreement.

I have a further argument, and tell him: my mother would have wanted me to go on without breaking down. I see he does not agree, but to keep me satisfied he does what I say.

9

Night falls. Grub arrives. They pass the list. We can go to bed. I curl up, and I drop into the night face to the wall, let myself be taken over by it, I want to lose myself in the night to think about my mother.

I'll never see her again. When I get out of prison she won't be there, never again, I won't be able to quarrel or laugh with her. It's impossible to get that idea into my head. I run through memories. It would take me years to organize those memories, images of that mother.

Among all the memories, I have one story she told me and it is the one that I love the most. My mother is a little girl, she lives in the country in a family with five brothers. To get to school she has to walk several kilometers. My mother has a pair of shoes for school that she can wear only in school. It is winter, rainy. My mother runs barefoot through the country. Carefully wrapped in her bag are her shoes. She gets to school, waits for her feet to dry, then puts on her shoes. When she gets out of school she wraps them back up, runs over the ground again to get home.

When I want to remember my mother I see her, a child, always laughing, running barefoot through the countryside in the rain, and I know that in her bag she carries her shoes.

10

Months later we reach the end of the Spanish language book. We do the last lesson at the proper hour. We correct the last exercise, unhurried, as should be, as we have done all along. We are serious people who take things seriously. The course is certainly serious.

When the pupil answers the last question I turn solemn and congratulate him.

He has earned the highest possible grade, and for that reason a celebration is declared in the school. We will not do anything more for the rest of the afternoon. From now on it will be his responsibility to use the knowledge he has acquired, read a lot, write letters to his daughter, not ever stop studying.

We clasp hands.

It's all a joke, but the two of us feel that we have beaten the prison at its isolation, the coarsening it has tried to impose on us. We are winners for now.

11

My father has been in bad shape since my mother's death. He drinks. He stops visiting me and sends my aunt, his sister, to visit. My sister is in Buenos Aires. Months later she takes him with her.

One day my father decides to come back. Having arrived in Montevideo, he puts on his suit and necktie. He visits our old neighborhood, chats with the neighbors. He is happy, conversational. All goes well.

The next day I am called to the visiting room. Odd, not my day for a visit.

There I learn that the day before, December 13, 1978, my father, after saying goodbye to his house, to the neighbors, and the neighborhood, killed himself.

I knew he was going to. He has told me so more than once.

"I don't want to live any longer without your mother."

I had no doubt he would commit suicide. What I wondered was when and how.

As soon as they tell me, I decide that nothing happened. I shut down, like a stone. Stay that way for years.

At night, in the dark, face to the wall, come memories, all night long.

But the pain shut up inside is not the only one. I also feel a great anger. I hate my father, I hate him for killing himself, for not thinking that I needed him, still need him.

Later, months, years later, I understand it was his act of love for my mother. His world had collapsed—without the woman with whom he had lived for twenty-eight years, son in prison, daughter in Buenos Aires, the sorrow of living in a country where having a son in prison was worse than carrying the plague. He couldn't endure any more, and chose to die. It was his courage, perhaps the most important moment in his life when he chose the day, the place, and the manner in which he would die. It was not a quiet death, or serene and painless. It was a terrible, painful death. He was fifty-four years old.

In 1985, when I was out of prison, I visited the place where my father killed himself. Not right after getting out, but a day when I felt strong and sure of myself. I went to the spot, looked at everything, tried to imagine. I understood the immense solitude weighing down on that man that day. I will dedicate to him all my tenderness, my gratitude for having worked to raise us. He was a good man. He took care of me, protected me. He did what a father ought. As the years pass, I'll know that looking after one's obligations is no small thing.

12

When I gather memories of my father, one in particular
stays with me. I am four years old. My father has a
cart, and a mare called Princesa. He gets up at one
in the morning and goes to the market to buy fruits
and vegetables. He gets back around seven, drinks hot
milk and coffee, and goes out into the street to sell his
merchandise, until evening.

In my memory it is winter, very early morning.
For some odd reason I am up, with my mother and
grandmother, at the front door. We are waiting for my
father. Suddenly on the dirt road the cart appears, going
very slowly. When it gets near I make out my father. He
comes wrapped in gunny sacks covered with hoarfrost.
He is a young man, under thirty, and my grandmother
and mother have to help him get down because he is
numb with cold. He goes into the kitchen. He drinks his
milk and coffee and leaves in his cart to work.

It is not a happy memory, it is just the one of him I
like best.

13

Now, without my parents, I begin to live in another world,
one in which I have no one behind me. From this point
on, without my parents, it is as though I have been left
alone on the planet. The entire responsibility for my life is
only mine, no one else's. Until now it has been possible to
lean back on them, if only mentally. Until now it has been
possible to blame them. Not now, neither leaning nor
blaming. My life is entirely mine, in prison or wherever it

might be, I am responsible for my acts, all of them. But I'll always feel the obligation to be loyal to the simple values they taught me, to their elemental dignity of working people.

Seven years later I would not be in Uruguay. Yet wherever I find myself where no one knows me, I'll know that even if I don't have to be accountable to anyone for my actions outside of myself, I should keep loyal to that little girl who runs through the countryside barefoot in the rain and to that man on a cart wrapped in gunny sacks, numb with cold. I also know I'd like there to be a spot on the planet where the remains of my parents rest, a place where one day I might go and speak with them, tell them their son is no longer a prisoner, thank them for the protection and care they gave me when I was little. Tell them, for good or ill, the son has got on, he lives. Tell them, who in the thirties could go no farther than third grade in school, that they produced a son dedicated to books. Or not tell them anything. Be able to say to myself: if you didn't bury your parents, at least you have carried out the obligation of visiting their tomb once in your life.

But I have never visited their tomb, I don't even know if they have one.

14

Police Headquarters in Montevideo, March 14, 1985. It's six, seven in the evening. A joyful and tense wait. We've been here for more than twenty-four hours. We are maybe thirty men, on the fourth floor. On the other side is a group of women waiting as we are. All of us have spent many years in prison, ten, twelve. Some, who went through more than one arrest, accumulated sixteen years.

We know they will free us tonight, but we don't know the time. We don't much care. We are used to waiting, waiting for anything. We've waited for all there is to wait for, now it is not our problem. It's their problem, they who are awaiting orders to let us go.

Even though the fourth floor is isolated almost at the center of the city block, we can hear shouting from the street: relatives, friends who arrived the previous night, sing, call greetings. The wind blowing through the hole of the patio brings snatches of those songs, letting us know they are waiting for us. The echo of these voices warms the heart. It was worth waiting so long.

Yesterday, after midday, they took us out of *Libertad* Prison. We walked in a line some three hundred meters to the gate, for the first time without our hands behind us, not forced to stare ahead or march in silence. They had us get on a bus.

We set out on the highway and there were several jeeps and trucks full of soldiers. All the way to Montevideo a helicopter followed. During the last days there were always people at the prison gates, relatives, friends, reporters. Yesterday there was only one car with relatives. When they saw us leave they realized who we were. The car took off, raced along the road and tried to get ahead of the convoy. As we entered Montevideo we saw it had crashed at a corner.

Many times over those years I had traveled from the prison to Montevideo always shut up in a truck and never saw the landscape. Now we could see the changes in the approaches to the city that we didn't know about. Suddenly I realized we were in La Teja, my neighborhood. The bus took Carlos María Ramírez Avenue. We went by the places I know best, my streets, two blocks from the house where I grew up, lived until I was twenty, a few meters from where my sister lives. Would my sister be home, not knowing I had passed so close?

15

On the fourth floor of Police Headquarters there is everything to talk about, and nothing. They have to set us free by midnight. That was what was decided, by law. Then liberty begins. At the moment we are in no-man's land, still prisoners.

They have us go down in small groups. Five days ago someone decided to organize the last football match in *Libertad* Prison before our liberation. I have played football since I was a child, and all through prison. Have had bones broken and often been in a cast. I did not want to play that day, didn't want anything to happen to me before I got out. But I had a duty to bid farewell in a game of football. And I sprained a toe.

16

The waiting goes on. Prisoners continue going downstairs to sign their release. After two or three hours, about half-past ten, things begin to move. They take us in a group of eight or ten to the basement of Police Headquarters, each with his bag. There a young officer speaks to us.

We'll be going in this truck like an armored car, with small windows. He explains they'll have a policeman inside, unarmed, whose mission is not to let anyone open the door from the outside. There are a lot of people in the street; it might be dangerous for us if they manage to get us out of the truck.

It's clear he has received orders. Each prisoner must be taken to the address he has given, and he must arrive safe and sound.

We are not at all interested in anything the officer is saying. He is nervous. Let him do what he wants, put on an armed, unarmed, or naked police guard. It's his problem. Those of us traveling in the armored car are old prisoners, accustomed to showing indifference to whatever they do, whatever garbage they say. Right now we are stronger than he is.

Those in the street are family, friends, people waiting for us; they won't harm us. But it's also true that I would not know what to do if they turned me loose in the crowd at the door of Police Headquarters.

Sitting inside the armored truck, the business of leaving is slow. We are used to that, too. More than used to, it would be astonishing if it were not that way. You always have to wait, that's what prison is about, waiting. Waiting for food, the visit, bathroom, going out to the patio, the package sent by relatives, liberty.

In prison, when night comes, the prisoner says, "One day less," so the other will answer, "One day more." All depends on how you look at it. If there is one day less to liberty, it's because one has been one day more in prison.

17

In the basement, inside the armored police truck, everyone is concentrating on his own affairs, as I am on mine. No one talks more than chitchat, a few people joke, we're nervous.

Suddenly everything starts up. The officer gives his last orders, gets in the first truck, and sits next to the driver, who starts the vehicle up the ramp that opens onto San José Street. One can hear shouting. Now things are in earnest. The truck behind starts, climbs up the exit hole out of the basement. Now we are on the sidewalk. Shouts, an immense shouting. The truck hits the street. People break the police barricade, throw themselves onto the truck, beat up on it. It resounds inside.

The vehicle makes a left turn on San José and takes off at top speed. We are outside. We are going to let the first man off at his house, among his people.

The truck runs all over the city. We arrive at the first house. There is light in the street. The rear door opens. Rodolfo gets down. He and I say goodbye as though we'll be seeing each other shortly. I manage to scan the street, the people. I don't distinguish details.

18

Round and round the city. I don't know where we are, nor much care. Somewhere in the suburbs. The truck stops in a street with little light, small low houses, poor people. A gathering on the corner. Another *compañero** gets off. Sudden shouts: "Assassins, assassins!"

They yell at the police. It leaves us indifferent. These police are following orders that we like. Calling them assassins may be overdoing it.

I don't know how many of us there were in the truck, how many of us went out that night. Odd, I didn't think to count, I who count everything set before me. I will never remember how many of us there were in that truck, nor do I particularly want to find out.

Suddenly I feel the strangeness of being a free man. For although I am going around in an armored police truck, with a policeman with a nightstick at the door, I am not a prisoner. I can do with my life what I want. It sounds beautiful, but is terrifying. Now what? What comes next? Impossible to ask anyone here, these fools thinking they are free.

If they were to drop me off just anywhere in the city, I wouldn't know what to do. I have no money, couldn't explain who I am, where I come from. It scares me. I want to get to somewhere familiar, among people I know.

Until yesterday I considered myself a strong individual, strong physically and mentally. Now I feel weak. I don't know what I'll do in society. I have no work, no position, no house, no identification documents. My friends are here, prisoners. All of us in the same boat.

I realize the worst is starting right now. When I arrive

---

*More than a "companion," a *compañero* is a friend and confidante who shares a colleague's political ideologies; they have possibly gone through periods of dangerous activism together. Before and during the dictatorship, the word was rather specifically associated with political resistance; since then it has acquired a looser and broader application, such as in reference to schoolmates, club members, or friends in general.

I will have to get identification, find work. My immediate plan: get to where I am going, greet people, and get started right away. I can't lose time.

For years in prison, liberty had been a white, infinite emptiness, in fading light. I could run toward it, could go in any direction I wanted, to the horizon. Stimulating, not desolate. Everything was possible, depending on my energy, my interests, my desire to advance.

Now liberty begins. And it isn't the empty space. It is this, a truck advancing through the city in the night, through streets and neighborhoods that I am not able to identify, that I may not know. It is not stimulating but disturbing, a challenge.

The prison was more comfortable: you couldn't do this, nor the other; there was barely anything you could do. If a meal arrives on time, you eat on time. If it arrives late, you eat late. And if it arrives neither on time nor late, you don't eat. This absence of choice is the sole remaining liberty, and no small thing. Others decide everything for me. I decide that I don't care what they decide. For the prisoner, to live is to resist one more day, one more night. For the free citizen, what does it mean to live?

All at once inside the truck I sense infinite liberty. I can choose any path I want, and that is enormous, immense, greater than any dream. The infiniteness of life is all before me. But that paralyzes me. Which path do I choose? When I choose one, I'll have lost all the others.

Thus liberty is an abstraction, nothing experienced. In a moment I shall have to begin deciding. I am already deciding, and cannot make any mistakes. It does not occur to me that first I should sit down and rest. Not at all. My thing is action, right now. Even this trip to liberty is a waste of time. I should be there now, doing something.

I am at the most difficult moment of my life. To move ahead I have the instincts of a woodland animal, a prisoner's habits of seeing without looking, hearing without listening, being aware without letting on.

19

On March 14, 1985, I recover my liberty. On December 11, 1985, I land in Stockholm.

On December 24, 1985, I am in Nená and Juanjo's house, Uruguayans. Juanjo was in prison; they've been in exile for years. It is my first Christmas Eve dinner since 1971. There are ten or twelve people around the table: daughters of Nená and Juanjo, and someone else I don't remember, plus a Uruguayan woman to whom they just introduced me.

The dinner goes on as one would expect on such occasions, with something special: a toast to Juanjo who is with his daughters after fifteen years, a toast to me, also free but far from my family. Juanjo and I are still getting used to life in society, in a country we don't know, where they eat things we have never tasted, with a snowy landscape beyond the window.

We've been through the solemnities proper to the day, and the courtesies of meeting again and celebrating the joy of freed prisoners. We are still at the table and the conversation begins to scatter, each group talking separately, telling stories, jokes.

Suddenly the woman opposite me, the Uruguayan I

don't know, laughs. A gush of laughter, like an explosion that fills the whole house. I stare at her. I look at her and think that what I am thinking cannot be, must be a fault in my memory.

I don't know this woman, nor do I even remember the name they told me an hour ago when we were introduced. Because I don't know her, and because I don't know whether it is appropriate, I don't dare ask her the question that comes into my head. In case she answers me no, I wouldn't know how afterwards to explain how I had confused her. In case she tells me yes, I would be going against what appear to me ordinary rules of politeness, not to bring up disagreeable subjects.

I can't help looking at her. She begins to notice. The situation is uncomfortable. Yes, I will ask her, but how do I put it?

In the midst of the babble I lean forward to speak to her so nobody else notices. I have the question planned in my head, which needs a preamble, an explication as to why, in case her answer be negative, she should not think I am crazy. As I am about to open my mouth to give her the explanation that introduces the question, I hear myself say, "You're the mad-dog woman!"

She looks at me and yells, "Yeeesss, I am the mad-dog woman."

It is the same tone of that scream that thirteen years ago came out of the torture room, reached the prison cells, cracked our heads apart. "And how do you know I am the mad-dog woman?"

"Because I was in the cell above."

Her voice makes it impossible for my question, and

her answer, to remain between the two of us as I had hoped.

In a loud voice, Olga begins telling her story, and what just took place between the two of us. When the military were interrogating her, besides torturing her, they threatened to kill her dogs. Like a good prisoner, she made the biggest fuss over the most minor issue to distract them from asking about major ones. Although she did not want them to kill her dogs, neither did she want to be asked anything else. She hoped to stop the torturers by making them think the threat of killing her dogs had unhinged her, and that she was crazy.

Every time they'd take Olga to the torture room we'd hear her scream, "Not the dogs! Not the dogs!"

My ear recorded that scream and that strident voice so exactly that I was able to identify her all these years later.

20

On November 1, 1986, in the evening, I am walking with Anna through the center of Stockholm, through the most beautiful island of the Swedish capital, that will later be my neighborhood for years, Sodermalm.

There is an ancient Protestant graveyard, with benches under shade tress, paths people take to their houses, and children going by on bicycles.

This evening the autumn cold is not as intense as it's apt to be here. I've been told of a custom of the country. On November 1, people go to the cemeteries and light a candle on the gravestones of their dead relatives, or of people they cared about. It is an act of piety, civilized, cultured.

When we get to the cemetery railing I tell Anna I want to go in. It is a small graveyard, not more than a square block, with a church to the side.

We go in as if to a park. In the shadows we see candles burning on the ground, on the tombstones, silhouettes of people moving quietly. We walk through the little graveyard. Anna talks about the customs of her country. I listen beside her, silently, with respect, knowing mine is partly a tourist's curiosity. Perhaps because my dead are not there, I can allow myself the distance of the curious.

For me, my dead are not in any place. I have gotten over their dying. I've never paid much attention to these kinds of ceremonies.

When we get to the center of the cemetery I stop at a gravestone. Someone has placed a candle and left it burning alone. I step closer. Anna is behind me. Then, without realizing it, without wanting to, I begin to cry.

I cry noiselessly, the tears run down my face. I try not to let Anna see, and keep my back to her.

I begin walking toward the exit. Anna follows me, silent. We leave the cemetery and walk and walk I don't know how many minutes. I know Anna has seen that I am crying. When I can I stop and beg her pardon. Anna passes her hand over my face, dries my tears.

I explain that I never thought this would happen to me. My mother died ten years ago, my father almost eight. I never cried, never felt the need to.

Then I realize that I'd like for there to be a spot, a

particular place for the remains of my parents, where I might go and say to them: forgive the delay, it was hard to get here, but here I am. I am out of prison.

21

April 1995. I've been in Montevideo for six months. I decide to go look for my parents. I don't know how that is done, don't know whom to ask.

I go to the Cemeterio del Norte. It is unlikely I'll find what I want. I tell the attending clerk my problem. I give him my parents' names, the dates they died.

Would it be possible to find them?

He does not know, but will see what he can do.

He opens an immense book where burials are entered by hand.

In a few minutes he has found them both.

It looks like I'm in luck. Normally, unclaimed remains are taken to the crematorium. In the case of my parents that has been delayed. We can still find them.

He asks me if I came by car.

I say I did.

We get in the car and go to a far end of the cemetery. We go into a storage area where there are hundreds of urns.

In spite of what the clerk said, I do not have much hope. Finding anything there is going to be difficult.

I walk along a corridor among stacked urns. In a few meters I see an urn among many with a metal plate: *Veremundo Liscano, 13-XII-1978.*

In that box are the bones of my father. My father is in

that box. I am nailed to the spot. The clerk gets to where I am.

Find something?

I point to the urn.

Well, now we have one.

We go out to find the other.

We go to a vault that is enclosed. The records say that my mother's remains are there. It has to be opened. A gravedigger appears. The clerk explains what we want, which urn we are looking for.

The gravedigger says he has a lot of work. He asks for a couple of days to open the vault.

Is it inconvenient for me to come another day?

No, not at all. I can come back anytime.

Friday?

Friday is fine.

22

Friday I go back to the cemetery. I look for the clerk who helped me. We get in the car. We go again to the place of a couple of days ago. When we arrive the gravedigger sees us and approaches. Next to a wall are two urns, the one I found and another that says *Ramona Fleitas, 31-V-1976.*

I squat and pass my hand over the urns. The two men are silent.

I stay there an instant, on my heels. I don't know what I'm thinking.

"Excuse me, I'm taking your time."

I'm not to worry.

"And now what do we do?"

They will be transferred to another place. There they may stay for twenty years.

The men won't let me carry the urns; they do so. They put them in the back seat of the car. I give the gravedigger a tip.

I start the car, the clerk beside me. In the back seat the bones of my parents. I repeat to myself: my parents are back there. Late, but I arrived. I have them; they are with me, I with them.

Later I give them over to another clerk, who puts them together, one next to the other, in another vault. I give out more tips, and get into the car.

I leave the cemetery and accelerate. I drive and drive, for kilometers.

Suddenly I stop. I am both empty and lucid. Although I know a writer is supposed to justify and intellectualize everything, I actually am able to say exactly what I feel at this moment. Albeit late, I have done my duty, the duty of burying my own dead. It was what I owed my parents, and myself. I feel a great peace. Although I have often thought I should do this, I did not know that doing so would bring me peace. Do my duty to them. Maybe only my duty to myself. I thought I had a lot of things to say to them and as it turned out, I had none. I only would have liked to see them once more, look them in the face.

Body and Self

1

I am backing up several years.

I am in prison in an army barrack. The torture
room is on the floor beneath the solitary cells. We
are seven prisoners, at most nine or ten. When they
put someone in the corridor *de plantón** and then
take him away, we become seven again. Always men,
never a woman. They say in another part of the same
barrack there is a group of sixty or seventy prisoners,
where men and women are mixed. We also know
there are prisoners in every barrack in the country,
at Police Headquarters in Montevideo, and maybe
even in scattered police stations. We also know that
some have died in torture. It is May 27, 1972, and there
are hundreds of us. In the coming years scores of
thousands will be tortured. The torturers will be—
how many?

---

*A form of torture in which a prisoner was kept in a rigid standing position,
hooded and naked in all weather, for hours or days, often with arms raised
and legs spread apart, causing leg swelling, bleeding, and sometimes delirium.
(*Uruguay Nunca Más, Human Rights Violations, 1972–1985,* compiled by
Servicio Paz y Justicia, 1989; translated by Elizabeth Hampsten for Temple
University Press, 1992.)

2

Everyone has an idea about torture. Obviously if one knows he might be arrested, he's thought about it. But no one can imagine the details. The details have to do with intimate knowledge of the body, not the human body in general, but one's own. Torture is like an illness, not everyone hurts the same, and only those who have gone through it know what it feels like.

Will torture be beatings, electric prods, impalement?

In the last weeks in Montevideo, before I got here, repression was in the air, you could touch it. Army, navy, air force, patrolling day and night, armed, threatening, fearful. Streets closed off, check-ups at all hours. Tense, violent atmosphere, a lot of violence. You could read it in the papers, hear it on the radio. Between April and May, almost twenty deaths. It is impossible not to think at any moment one may be arrested and tortured. It is impossible not to think about how one will endure torture.

Before I was arrested, I thought the best I could do was to break down. Endure until couldn't stand any more, and then they could not torture an inert body. But I have an advantage I had not thought of: I am twenty-three years old, healthy, with a strong heart. Later torture will make me think my age and good health are disadvantages. If my heart gave out in the middle of torture, I'd die, and that would be the end of it. But my heart does not fail me; it is the heart of a strong young man active in sports all his life.

In torture one wants die, begs the torturer to kill. The torturer says, "You want us to kill you. But we won't."

3

Death in torture was not the torturers' object, but neither was much done to avoid it, nothing of what they might have done. They killed whom they pleased, with a single shot, or threw him in the river, or from a rooftop. The means did not matter, they killed because they decided to kill. But death in torture was not planned. That does not absolve torturers from responsibility, nor lessen the blame. There was always a group of doctors on hand who'd tell them how far they could go, when to stop and let the prisoner rest. But the torturer would not consult with the doctor before starting his work. Nor would he ask the prisoner if he had any "contraindications" against torture. That is not in the ontology of the job. Death in torture does not happen by accident, but by the savagery and negligence of the torturer, his superior officers, the doctors. Military doctors are not trained in military quarters, but in the university. One might ask how the same university that trains doctors who die in torture can also train those who help to torture.

4

The night is noisy and chaotic. Torture begins about ten or eleven o'clock, rarely during the day. At night you hear men and women screaming, dogs barking to terrify prisoners. The officers also shout, threaten, yell insults. After awhile in the cells one can sleep even with the desperate cries of the tortured.

The torture room smells of dampness and tobacco. As a workplace it is inhospitable and insalubrious. There is a two-hundred-liter metal tank, cut in half, full of water. The prisoner, male or female, enters the room, led in with shoves and blows. Torture has not begun yet; this is only to frighten, the "loosening up" process.

There is a good torturer and a bad one. The good torturer advises the prisoner that he does not like to torture, but that his partner is a very tough, violent guy, of few words, able and willing to do the worst.

To demonstrate, the bad torturer makes himself understood. If it were left to him, the prisoner would soon learn how things work around here.

But the good one has not yet given up on his kindly method, and continues arguing. He does not approve of torture. But if the prisoner does not talk to the good guy, he won't be able to help turning him over to his partner, who is a very bad character. If the prisoner chooses, all may be worked out without violence. All he has to do is answer what he's asked.

In any case the prisoner must know that if he does not cooperate they will get the information anyway, which is the purpose of the bad one. Therefore, it is better for the prisoner and for them to avoid rough treatment and torture, right? So start off without violence. Because, the prisoner should know, they have all the time in the world to extract information. Is the prisoner willing to cooperate?

The prisoner is bewildered, but his head is working at high speed. He can't pretend to be tough, and must think of plausible answers to possible questions. He also might go purposefully delirious, right there, right away, from the beginning. And then keep up the delirium for days, weeks, months. That is difficult and dangerous.

The prisoner does not choose delirium. He chooses another sinuous and dangerous path that he does not know where will lead, but which he thinks he can follow with resistance and cunning. With courage?

The prisoner promises cooperation.

Good, if he wants to cooperate, then he should tell all he knows.

Next comes the dis-intelligence between the torturer and the prisoner. Because the prisoner says that he wants to cooperate, but does not know anything.

The prisoner and the officer are playing the same game. The prisoner wants to know how much the interrogator knows about him, and for that awaits the question that will orient him. If the question has nothing to do with him, he'll feel relieved. If the question has some relation to him, with his activities, or if he has information that might help the torturer, the prisoner will try to develop an answer that gives the minimum of information. He has seconds to think of something likely and convincing that does not give out any information that the torturer does not already have. Actually it's better to wait, keep on refusing, everything, until the torturer asks a specific question, and so be able to work out a specific lie that looks true.

The torturer insists that to save time and unpleasantness for both parties the prisoner should tell all he knows.

Now we are getting to the end.

The dialogue, or whatever you want to call this, ends at last when the prisoner repeats that he knows nothing.

The good torturer gets annoyed, or acts annoyed, and gives his place to the bad one. The bad one hits him, gives him a kick. The prisoner does not know whether it is the good or the bad who is beating up on him, but supposes it is both.

The torturers—there are always four or five—bring the prisoner up to the edge of the tank of water. One sticks his hand in and removes it.

Does the prisoner hear the water? Well, if he does not talk, that's where he'll go.

After a while, long or short, the torturer gets bored and tries to put the prisoner in the tank. It's not an easy task. The prisoner resists. Then begins the softening up of the stomach muscles. From the blows, the prisoner doubles over with pain and then is plunged headfirst into the tank.

This lasts, how long? Impossible to tell. For the prisoner it is an eternity.

5

Thanks to blows to the stomach, when the prisoner is ducked in the tank he has no air in his lungs. He is hooded and handcuffed behind. He swallows water, feels he's drowning. That is what it feels like, choking to death.

When they take him out of the tank, the cloth hood is full of water. So a hand closes the hood around his neck, and the water takes time to drain out. The drowning sensation goes on for seconds longer. The prisoner yells and yells. They are not normal cries of pain, but bestial, like a desperate animal. His nose and mouth cannot get enough air. The sound comes out in gasps, a succession of explosions. It's a bellow more than a shout. The body moves, jerks. There is no air anywhere.

6

Two struggles face the prisoner, both unequally matched. One is against the torturers, who are many, who can do anything, and the prisoner is defenseless. He can't even count on his whole body to defend him, for he has no use of his hands, can't see, barely breathes. Time, exhaustion, physical pain—all wear against him. In this contest the prisoner has nothing to gain and everything to lose. With physical and mental strength, and luck, and rage, and hate, maybe tonight he might make it. But the next time?

The torturer, however, does not have everything in his favor. Even though he shouts repeatedly, "We have all the time in the world to get information out of you," the prisoner knows, that is not so. As long as the prisoner resists and time passes, the information he has loses currency, is no longer useful. Facts the prisoner might give tonight that would lead to the arrests of others, won't be any good by dawn. The torturer is in a hurry, that is his disadvantage.

The torturer also gets into a bad humor, tires, sweats, gets dirty, gets fed up, starts drinking, loses control, beats for the sake of beating, unprofessionally. And another thing against him—he spends the night torturing, or in the street arresting people, breaking into houses where there are families, women, children, and has no time to look after his house, his own family.

Years later I would hear a story that I don't know is true. A young officer in my barrack, recently married, patrols the streets at night. He feels like going by his house to see his wife, who is young, alone, and whom he has not seen in several days. The woman does not know her husband is coming. The young officer orders the driver to stop in front of his house. He gets out of the car. Opens the door. Enters. The woman is in bed with a lover. The officer takes out his pistol and kills the man.

The prisoner's other unequal struggle is with himself. Talk or not talk. In either case he loses, as there is no way to win at this game. If he does not talk, torture and the suffering continue, the prisoner does not know for how long. If he believes he can stay firm on his feet to the end, but can't, and breaks down, it could be disastrous, could lead to his giving out all the information he has without resistance, without making the torturer pull it out.

If the tortured prisoner talks, he will be faced with his worst enemy, be left alone with himself, for weeks, months, years, thinking he is shit, asking himself why, telling himself he should and could have stood more, a little more, one more night, another session, another dunking of his head in the tank.

7

When he is in the water, the prisoner exerts strength he does not normally have, kicks his legs, moves his torso, bangs his head against the side of the tank. The officers, two of them, have to hold him while he is in the water so he does not hurt his head, so he does not go all the way down to the bottom. If he does go down to the bottom, a heavy body is hard to lift out, and the prisoner may drown. It's a matter of seconds. An instant of distraction and a corpse is removed from the water.

When they do take him out, the prisoner lashes out desperately, hitting whoever is holding him without meaning to. Tough job, torturing—takes strength, resolution, self-forgetfulness.

I am more than a meter and eighty centimeters tall, weigh almost eighty kilograms. Am a mass of flesh and bones not easy to manage. Not even when a body no longer struggles, when it is dead flesh, is it easy to move such a shape and weight.

A certain lieutenant, short in stature, little more than a meter and fifty centimeters, has made himself famous as a torturer inside and outside Uruguay. One night when they take me out of the tank they let me fall to the floor and this lieutenant starts kicking me. I am aware they are beating up on me, and that my wrists in the handcuffs behind me are suffering, but they don't hurt. What I am after just then is seeking air, air, all the air in the world. They have to grab the lieutenant to stop him kicking me.

It is not normal to be beaten up on the floor after coming out of the tank. The reason for the kicking, I learn later, is that the little lieutenant was assigned, along with one other, the job of dunking me in the tank. I was too tall and strong for him, and while kicking head-down in the tank, I kicked him in the face. He got furious. When they take me out, he loses it and kicks me, hooded and handcuffed, on the floor.

8

It's June, winter, cold. After torture sessions, handcuffed behind his back, the prisoner is placed *de plantón* facing the wall, legs far apart, in the cell or in the corridor. The toes swell, legs swell, the back can barely remain upright.

Wrists hurt from the tight handcuffs, lose feeling,

first the thumbs, then other fingers, the whole hand. The handcuffs are designed to squeeze on their own accord. If the prisoner tries to loosen up he gets the opposite effect, they will tighten until they dig into the flesh. Best leave them the way they are. But in the struggle during torture, the handcuffs tighten of their own accord. Useless to beg to have them loosened, no one will pay attention, but actually it's better they be tight. That hurts permanently and so works at softening up.

In time the handcuffs begin to make a flesh wound. Loss of feeling in my thumb continued a long time after I finished with torture, years.

If the prisoner is left too weak, they dump him on a mattress. There he will stay until they come for him again. Because here, the prisoner does not yet know, everything can start all over again at any time.

9

The water in the tank is dirty and smells bad. The prisoner may vomit in the water, leave saliva, hair, false teeth. The job of torturer is not an easy one. It takes a lot of strength to put an individual head-first into the tank. Once there, the prisoner flays his legs, makes desperate efforts not to drown. When they take him out his body is wet from head to crotch, the water runs down his legs to his feet. The officers also get wet. The environment in the torture room is tumultuous at times. To the howling of the prisoners add the shouts of the torturers. It smells of tobacco, sweat, alcohol, urine, disinfectant from the toilet. It smells of human misery, an indefinable odor that

inundates torture rooms the world over. Here it smells
of two kinds of misery: that of the person tortured and
that of the torturers. They are not the same, these odors.
Neither are the miseries, but they affect the same animal.

10

The body tries to adapt to any situation. No one knows
when he will be taken to the torture room and tries to
prepare himself for when his turn comes. One should
eat everything served up, rest even when *de plantón*, sleep
even when wet, hooded, and handcuffed behind the back.
Perhaps the worst feeling is being lifted up violently from
sleep to be dunked in the tank two minutes later. You can't
prepare, don't know what they will ask this time, whether
the same questions will be repeated or the torturers have
gotten new information to ask new questions.

Sometimes when they have no one to interrogate,
nor know what to ask, torturers do "a review." The review
consists in torturing again the same prisoners who have
been interrogated dozens of times. Torturers ask about
anything, "just in case." As they don't know what to ask,
they ask at random.

After a few torture sessions the prisoner can tell
when the torturers are sure of themselves, when they are
groping, and when it is a "review" and not an interrogation
"for real." Torture is more bearable in the reviews.
Torturers get bored and look for someone else, and then
another someone else.

11

Each prisoner is assigned a *responsable*, a person who
"responsible" or in charge of him, usually a captain
if the prisoner is "important." Lieutenants and
second lieutenants take charge of prisoners of "minor
importance."

The *responsable* is the prisoner's owner: perhaps not
of his life, because to kill intentionally he is supposed to
get permission, but he is the owner of everything else.
The prisoner is the property of his *responsable*. In my
case, I am the property of a captain who arrested me. My
captain has illusions of being just.

"If you give me the information I want, I shall treat
you well."

It is up to me for the captain to be able to
demonstrate his feeling for justice.

He's not original; they all say the same.

My captain is a little older than I am, perhaps thirty.
He's a little heavy, shorter than I am, taciturn, with a
thick voice. Smokes all the time. Sometimes gives me a
cigarette.

The ownership of the prisoner by the *responsable* is
absolute. The prisoner sleeps the hours the *responsable*
decides, eats if the *responsable* wishes, is handcuffed in
front or behind as the *responsable* decides, will have a
blanket if the *responsable* orders it. The *responsable* is "his"
owner, but both belong to each other. The prisoner has
just one owner, the *responsable* may own several prisoners
at a time.

As the *responsable* directs the torture of his prisoner,
he gets to know him intimately. He sees him at his worst,

which is when you know a human being to his depths. He sees him suffer, hears him scream, feels his useless resistance of a trapped animal. When the prisoner begs to breathe, that they not beat him, asks to go to the bathroom, lies, invents, humbles himself, the *responsable* is there. When the prisoner is wounded flesh, wet with urine, smelling bad, a soaking rag on a filthy pad, the *responsable* is there. To the *responsable* nothing about the prisoner is unfamiliar.

12

I don't know whether the *responsable* is made any better by this authentic and profound knowledge, like going into the deepest parts of a being with a little light in hand. I don't know whether knowing me in this way makes mine better. At any rate I doubt it leaves him indifferent.

When I meet him, now in the prison years later, and he wants to converse with me and offers me a chair, and I refuse to accept it and remain standing, and he calls me *tú*, while I use the formal address,* and he asks after my health, my family, if I sleep well, eat well, receive correspondence, it gives me the impression he has reflected.

Perhaps it is only my desire that my beaten-up body, and those of so many others, has done my *responsable* some good. It is an anachronistic desire and stupid, and

———

*Tú (you) is the informal, intimate form of second-person address, appropriate in speaking to children, families, friends, and social inferiors. Usted is the more polite form among adults, or in addressing superiors.

there is not even time to express it, but it could be stated like this:

I hope that the suffering he caused me rouses in him even a thousandth of the reflections it provokes in me to know there are human beings like him. That when he gives in to cancer, as he will and as I know he did years later, when I will have been a free individual who continues seeking liberty, my *responsable* can enjoy adding to his death each of the deaths that now he is making me die, choking in that tank. It is not vengeance, not irony, not a joke. I wish it on him, that he not die without having known himself in the end. That that was how he was.

13

A good *responsable* looks after his prisoner. He does not let others torture him, or a soldier on guard hit him for no reason. A good *responsable* is a little paternalistic with his prisoner; he never tortures beyond what is necessary. He is jealous; does not allow anyone of the same or lesser rank to interfere with *his* prisoner.

Sometimes, in the early morning, the *responsable* takes a little time to converse with his prisoner in his cell about matters not directly related to information about the repression. He asks after the family, who they are, how many there are, what they do. He also lets the prisoner in on his own feelings, his social and political concerns. The *responsable* might speak of his origins, say he too belongs to the people. He might even let the prisoner know he is not totally in agreement with the form of interrogation, but is not the boss. From which the prisoner should understand that from a certain point of view, the two are victims of the same mistaken decisions of his superiors.

After these confessions, is there anything special the prisoner needs? Nothing? Good, then the *responsable* will leave, he has things to do. There may be some other man or woman *de plantón* in another part of the barrack, waiting for the *responsable* to interrogate him—and wishing the *responsable* would break a leg, be killed by a shot in the stomach, that the barracks would blow up and everyone with it—the *responsable*, officers, soldiers, dogs—except the prisoner, and thus the prisoner will be able to run out and go home to welcoming hands, to liberty.

14

The fact of the *responsable* lends an order to things, to the barracks and also to the prisoner. The *responsable* is the prisoner's reference point, a mixture of authoritarian and punishing father, slave-owner, and minor god, who doles out pain, food, water, air, clothing, personal hygiene, trips to the bathroom. The *responsable* is a necessary person to this world of pain.

No one denies the importance of the *responsable*. However, there are people who disagree and don't think the *responsable* is everything, nor can cover all parts of his prisoner's life.

After a time in the barracks, the prisoner and his *responsable* have developed a relationship in which the *responsable* is treating the prisoner with certain condescension—or maybe not condescension so much

as that the *responsable* no longer is seeing the prisoner
objectively. He thinks he knows everything about his
prisoner, but suspects the prisoner is hiding an important
part of his life, of his activities. So for a night the rules
are changed, and prisoners under suspicion are separated
from their *responsable* and interrogated by someone else.

Thus some ten prisoners are tortured severely, at
half an hour per prisoner, which takes all night. It is not
possible for a single group of torturers to endure five
hours of torture. A prisoner can take it, not a torturer.
That's why there are shifts. Although all the torturers will
be in the room, each will direct the interrogation of only a
single prisoner who is not his.

15

In these special sessions, new information always comes
up. Perhaps not new, but something that allows torturers
to make connections among items they already had but
that they had not understood well, or located, or come to
conclusions about. It is hard to know who is who when
every prisoner has a pseudonym, and sometimes more
than one. If only to clear up pseudonyms, the sessions can
be useful.

On such a night of truth, the emotional relationship
between the prisoner and his *responsable* is put to the test,
and further confirms the oddness of their relationship.
If the special session gives no result, the *responsable* is
assured he can trust his prisoner. But if under brief
and intense torture the prisoner gives information his

boss does not know, the relationship deteriorates. The *responsable* feels betrayed, which confirms that there is something special between the two, something that breaks down when he discovers his prisoner has been lying to him. The *responsable* gets irritated, scolds his prisoner for not having given him the information, for making him look bad in front of his colleagues and superiors.

For several days the *responsable* shows his prisoner he has done something unforgivable. He does not come at dawn through the cellblock to exchange words, nor offer a cigarette. He does not treat him as before.

But because the *responsable* is paternal, and therefore understanding, in the course of the following days he'll show his prisoner he's forgiven. But he'd better not do it again, next time he'd better give all the information he has to him, or the *responsable* will never trust the prisoner again.

16

In the cell block there is a bathroom. To be allowed to urinate is a constant objective. Soldiers who guard prisoners have their rhythm, perhaps orders, and don't take prisoners to the toilet when they ask. They take their time. Although they aren't doing more than sitting there, they don't answer the prisoner's request. So the prisoner starts asking to go to the bathroom long before he feels desperate. That way, he might be allowed to urinate before he can't hold off any longer. The effort can become counterproductive. The soldier gets bothered, decides to punish the pest, and won't take him to the bathroom for several hours.

If the prisoner insists too much, he runs the risk that when the soldier goes off duty he will say to the entering soldier, "Don't take this one to the bathroom. He's acting up."

Perhaps it's all because the soldier is under great pressure, has been on guard for hours, sleeps little, is not allowed to go home, and for any slight error or negligence may receive a heavy sanction. He'd rather not take any initiative, stay quiet. To take a prisoner to the bathroom (three meters away), the soldier has to take off his handcuffs from behind and put them in front, and then change them back again. This annoys the soldier, and may include a degree of danger. Result: he does not take the prisoner to the bathroom. The prisoner waits, and finally, wanting to or not, urinates on himself. In the winter cold, urine running down his legs and wetting his pants gives an instant of pleasure. The heat of the urine, although he knows it will leave a smell and irritate his skin, relieves both cold and bladder.

To defecate is a more complicated objective. It must be done hooded, into an invisible hole in the floor. Handcuffs are switched to the front. Then the soldier takes off the handcuffs when the prisoner finishes so he can wipe himself. Then puts them on again, at the back. Many operations.

Although it hardly matters because the hood does not let him see, the prisoner knows the toilet has no door and that the soldier is there, leaning against the doorframe, watching him or conversing with another soldier. Over the years the prisoner gets used to doing this in public, anywhere, even in a plaza full of people, but here in the barracks, he still holds onto old habits and wishes for privacy.

As the difficulties are so many, prisoners would rather not defecate. Then they get diarrhea or become constipated. The last is my trouble; I go four weeks, five, six, without being able to defecate.

17

The prisoner under torture holds out because of the body's infinite capacity for resistance. If the body does not resist, he dies. End of torture.

But before that, stronger and more necessary than the body's ability to endure pain, something else sustains the prisoner. It is not ideology, not even ideas, nor does it affect all the same or equally. The prisoner holds onto something beyond the rational, the definable. Dignity sustains him. Maybe not even the dignity of the political activist, but a more primitive sense of dignity, consisting of simple values, learned who knows when, perhaps at home at the kitchen table when a child, or on schoolroom benches, or at work. It is not an abstract but a very specific dignity, that of knowing that one day he will have to look in the face of his children, his mate, his companions, his parents. Even if it's not so many people, it's enough to want someday to feel dignity before just one. For those eyes he resists, for that look in the future he buries himself in his misery and gathers his forces, yells, lies, wants to die to lessen the pain, and wants to live to remember one day that even in torment he held onto the dignity he was taught, remember that he never trusted the torturer, hated him, was capable of killing him with his bare hands, bathing in his blood, and destroying him until not even the dust of his bones remained.

Because loathing, pure loathing, also sustains, helps pass the night, another night, endure successive deaths in the tank, the cries of other prisoners.

After fifteen years out of prison, some nights the nightmare returns, although gradually less often. I am at home and they come to arrest me. I know they are there, at the door, and will come in. I jump from the bed, look for a gun. I hate them, hate them to the end. Never, never again will they come to take me to prison, I won't go back to the hood, the sessions in the tank, the disgust at my own body. I don't want to kill them, but will make them kill me.

I look and look and don't find anything. I have no guns, I live among books and papers. I despair. I don't want to escape, I couldn't, there are many of them, they are there, the house is surrounded. If I can't find a gun I can't make them kill me, and they will take me.

And I wake up and am afraid. Not afraid of them, but of me, of my feelings, this hatred, so old, so deep that still lives somewhere inside me. And I think: Is this me? Am I like this? Able to do this? I ask my body if it is he who has not been able to forget.

Dawn comes and I know I do not hate them, don't wish them dead; I only feel contempt for them. But in a few months, a year, again the fear will come back, and in the dream I again will decide, without thinking, without ever having thought about it lying awake, that it is better to die, than to feel again the disgust at my own body, a filthy animal, urinated on, flesh degraded by the garrote.

18

We do not bathe, do not shave. The body smells. Not that one pays much attention to the odor. There are other things to worry about: be tortured the least amount possible, not give out any information to torturers, eat, rest, sleep. But sometimes, during the day, when there is no torture, you smell sweat, saliva stuck to the beard and hood, your own and others' hair inside the hood from dunking in the tank, the smell of urine, the bad odor of weeks without brushing teeth. Disgust of the body varies from one individual to another. Some can stand their own odors better than others. In any case you get used to them. Or not, but know you can't afford to worry about the smell of your own body.

19

The prisoner has other, more important problems, or just one: torture. Torture means trying not to talk, forgetting everything one knows. But it is not wise to think complete forgetfulness is possible, because when least expected, in torment, memory returns. So you don't try to forget so much as to put information away in the most hidden part of the brain, and shut it up from intrusion by pain, pain that can force an opening to the spot where what the torturer wants to know is hidden.

But, if pain succeeds in opening the place of hidden information, I'd better organize answers to possible questions. If they ask me this, I'll answer that. So-and-so I don't know. The other I've known since we were children, I have no political relationship with her, only friendship.

That is how the prisoner spends his time, although sometimes he can't keep his thoughts from running to what he consciously does not want to think about: pleasant memories, relatives not recently heard from. And one constant: if I escape, where do I go where they won't find me? The mind wanders, converses, hears voices. When it realizes it is delirious, the prisoner tries to concentrate on the one thing that matters: torture to come, words to swallow.

20

The body is subjected to asphyxia in the tank, to beating, and to its own filth. These are absolutely new sensations for the body. Many years later, sick, without being able even to move my arms, I would realize how physical pain is a door to self-knowledge. When I am sick I learn there are things about me I don't know and that are similar to torture: the limit where one is capable of giving anything to relieve the pain, the sense that nothing is nearer, more important, or dearer than the body itself.

Bodily odor can be caused by torture or illness. The first thing one wants is for pain to stop, all the rest is secondary. The sick person can do no more than wait for the results of medical treatment. But for the person tortured, relief depends on himself or herself. Only talk, and torture will stop. And so the struggle begins: talk to avoid pain, carry the guilt of betraying companions. So as long as he can, he chooses pain, and knows he is obliging his body to suffer, to resist, to let him face himself with dignity.

But the pain, when will it stop?

It depends on the torturers, they will decide the moment when not to interrogate a prisoner—man or woman—any longer. But the pain also depends on the prisoner: all he has to do is turn over the information wanted for the pain to stop. But then conscience returns: this pain will pass, eventually it will pass. He begs a little more of the body, another bit, another night. Because one day the body will get over the pain. The other pain is forever, to be lived with.

21

Filth is another door to self-knowledge. Bad smells, urine on clothing, spit and leavings of food stuck to the beard, hair stiff from not being washed for weeks, skin beginning to shed for lack of sun and washing, all this brings on loathing. No one would put up with someone in such a state next to him. But one has to put up with his own self. This body, dirty, smelling bad, in pain from beatings and from lack of rest, sleepy, that can't so much as move a foot without asking permission, provokes disgust. It's one thing to think, "This is disgusting." It's different to feel, "Now I am disgusting."

But one can't ask the body to bear pain and at the same time tell it is disgusting. You feel for this animal.

It's disgusting but one wants to love it, because it is all one has, because dignity depends on its resistance, some dignity. Because what the torturer wants is for the prisoner to feel disgust toward himself. That he is so defenseless that he thinks he's worth nothing, and therefore keeping his mouth shut, lying, resisting, will cease to make sense. If one is not worth anything, if one is disgusting, what has he got to defend in the torment? Not even future memories.

I don't know how to explain how far disgust toward one's own body goes before one sees himself differently, and that that knowledge is for life. It is a dimension I don't think is provided by normal life, the recognition of the animal in oneself—the animal one is, always has been, at any moment may return to being, by choice or obligation.

Years later I would see and think of my body as a friendly animal. For that I have to thank the disgust I once felt for it when I realized I could not endure it but it was all I had, and I had better go on loving it, caring for it, protecting it. Love the animal that one is, to keep on being human.

22

Such conditions provide another source of knowledge about human beings—the officers who torture, get drunk, yell, sweat, get dirty dunking and lifting prisoners out of the water. When they go home, what do they tell their wives, their girlfriends, children, parents, and friends? The torturer is the same as oneself, speaks the same language, shares the same values and prejudices. Where does he come from? How does an individual become that?

There is the soldier who follows orders one after another, all the same to him. The soldier is not responsible, his superiors are the ones who turn him into a villain. But one can find a soldier doing things that were not ordered. The hooded prisoner is always led, so sometimes as a joke, a soldier has a prisoner run head-on into a wall. As the prisoner cannot even grope because his hands are tied behind his back, he hits the wall with his forehead or his face. The blow is not severe, but the surprise is disagreeable and makes it hurt a lot more than it ought.

The soldier says, "Ah, pardon." And one knows he did it so another soldier will see. They both laugh.

One asks, therefore, why does the soldier do what was not ordered, what is not even torture for information, but plain evil, with no point, no objective. The soldier does not know who the prisoner he's leading is, nor what his name is, does not even know whether he might be in prison by mistake and freed in a week. He has him beaten, or beats him, for mere diversion. One has been used to thinking that all human beings are alike, and now has to ask, how is it that this particular human being, the soldier, can make a totally defenseless individual bang his head against the wall?

These are new truths learned in torture: the disgust one feels toward his own body, the officer who tortures while claiming to be just, the soldier who thinks it's funny for the prisoner to hit his head against a wall. That is also the human being.

23

I don't pretend to be an innocent who does not understand and never understood violence, for I once was among the thousands of Latin American youths who believed that hunger, misery, exploitation, the preventable deaths of newborns, could only be eradicated with counter-violence. Now I no longer believe so, but have no right to deny the past, at least mine, for which only I am responsible.

But at present, when all I can do is try to save myself from torture with as much dignity as possible, I am not disposed to thinking so far ahead.

Yet, thirty years later I am not looking to the side and denying the old violence in which I participated, nor not seeing the new. I still believe there are times one has the right to resist, to rebel violently against violence, against misery and lack of liberty.

Although sometimes I may doubt, I'll never stop believing in a human being's shining capacity for indescribable acts of loyalty and sacrifice. But I also know human beings are capable of absolute evil, of hurting others for sport, of allowing a person to die in torment. Before I became a prisoner I did not know that such infinite degradation, such a descent to the abyss, was possible. It is scary to look at oneself in the mirror. Those things I learned in solitary prison cells.

24

I have time to indulge myself in memories of happy moments with my parents, my sister, friends. I don't realize I am little more than a boy, I haven't lived nearly as much as I thought, an idea that will come to me some years later. What I feel now is that my memories are few, and I keep going back to the same ones, not only because they are pleasant, but because I have no others. Maybe, in spite of my few years, I could have had more memories, but did not take advantage of all that was possible before now.

Thoughts fly, I make plans, beautiful plans. If I were free tomorrow I'd go home and take time to show my family how much I love them. I would like to do what I could have done and didn't, finish what I started and abandoned, repair what I did badly. I'd like to have books, read, learn. I know all there is to learn, and know I know nothing. I wish this moment would be over, now, to start over, study, learn. Above all, to begin writing. But to write you have to read a lot. Until a few weeks ago I thought one day I would have time to read, and then start writing. Write about what? I don't know, can't think of anything. It's less than a plan, a dream.

Maybe I could do with a lot less. It would be enough to walk along the street. If I could do that I would look differently at the landscape, at people, places. I would not run by paying no attention. I'd focus on details. Even though I know the city fairly well, there are places I have never been, and now I am curious to see them.

This situation, torture, is a passing thing. Afterwards,

I'll return to normal. What is "normal" for me? I don't know, don't ask myself, I can't. But it does not occur to me that torture and prison will be forever, or that one day I'll end up writing about this, about this misery. I know my life would be unimaginable for me without this one that I am living, without the thirteen years I will have lived it. I have said to myself, not once but many times, with a primitive conviction that goes beyond literature, beyond the more or less acquired skill of stringing words together, that if another life had been possible, I would not have chosen it.

I might also travel, know other countries, other people, take up language courses again. By this time I am delirious, traveling nowhere, stretched out on the mattress. I am aware I am delirious, but don't want to stop, don't want to go back to the cell, to this barrack, to the pain of knowing that my family must be suffering for me, that I am twenty-three years old, ignorant, will go on being ignorant, a poor beast who does not work, does not study, does not progress. I want to keep on fantasizing, fly away, not be me if only for awhile, think all is smooth, agreeable, that I am home, in a house, sitting in the midst of books, studying, writing.

25

When they have a little free time, the officers like to explain and defend their activity.

They are not professional torturers, but rather individuals like anyone else—fathers, sons, brothers.

They don't deny there is misery and injustice. In time, they will fix all that.

It's all the fault of the country's politicians, all of them corrupt liars and thieves.

They and we are victims of the system that created the politicians.

Torture is the only tool they have for getting information.

Torture has been part of every war, etcetera.

Then other times, some nights, torturers show a curious aspect: envy of the prisoners. Because deep down the torturer knows that never will what he does have any dignity, any human, cultural, moral, or ethical value. Suppose they get the information they want, then what? They may succeed in having every man and woman in the country afraid of them—in the street, in factories, in the university—who until they lock up the house and go to bed at night, will fear the torturer. Then what? Will that make the torturer feel proud? Never, not in a thousand years will he be proud to say to his children, "There was a man, or a woman, with information he did not want to give me. He was hooded, handcuffed behind his back. He refused. But I took him to the limit, smashed him, broke him down. Made him feel he was garbage. Made him feel what death was like under water, once, many times, and in the end he gave me the information."

26

Those nights, with a little alcohol, the torturer talks, and shows another aspect of his envy, how little he values himself. He envies the prisoner for his ideas, his relationships, his political loyalty. He envies his knowledge, his culture, the books he's read. He envies the woman who is his partner and also in prison, or underground.

Not only envy and resentment motivate the torturer, there are also his orders, respect for hierarchy, his training, the state, other people's economic interests. Envy and resentment show up in his futile desire to make the prisoner feel worthless, his efforts to degrade his victim. He does not say so, but the prisoner understands, feels it in his bones.

At night you can hear soldiers making comments about the women in another part of the same barrack, whether they are pretty, that they've seen them half-naked in the bath, or in torture, their legs, breasts. Theirs is a variation of the officers' envy, coarser, more vulgar. But the officers could say the same of women prisoners. Although they don't want to, sometimes a remark escapes them. One officer even tries to be alone with a woman prisoner, tells her she is beautiful, confesses he likes her, he'd like to go to bed with her, that if she agreed he'd see to it she was not mistreated any more, or he'd get her transferred to a better place.

In any case, before "important" prisoners, officers want to be seen to have their own political ideas, every one of them a future statesman, torturers but honest, brutal but cultured, crude but educated.

27

Death is an ever-present idea as a solution to unbearable torture. I think up a way out, as unfortunately I am not likely to die of heart failure, nor be allowed to drown in the tank. I could try an escape and have myself shot. After thinking about it for days, I've decided that's what I'll do.

In the next session I let myself be put in the tank a couple of times. I have to make it look like they are getting information because of torture and not because I have decided to collaborate.

When they take me out, I offer to turn over a contact. I tell them the place, a busy street, and the hour.

Who is it? What's the name of the contact?

I tell them the contact has been established, but I don't know who will be going. In any case, it is someone I know.

What does he look like?

I tell them I don't know, but I do know the partner who will be going to the contact.

It doesn't sound to me like a very well developed story, but it's the best I can do, all my head is good for.

I don't tell them that if they take me I could point him out and they could arrest him, because they might suspect I intend to escape. It will have to be they who make the suggestion. And even then I'll have to show a certain reluctance.

They stop torturing, which at first is a step ahead of what things were. But if they realize that I have no contact on that street that day, the result will be disastrous for me.

They take me to my solitary cell.

In a little while the captain comes by, my *responsable*. He is a little annoyed, or acts annoyed, because I had not given him that information before.

Am I sure that contact exists, I'm not making them go for nothing?

Yes he exists, of course he does.

I should pay close attention. My *responsable* trusts me, as I well know. But if I've lied, I'll have lost all the trust that I had earned.

No, it's the truth, I swear.

Then comes the question I wanted: was I willing to take them to the contact and identify the *compañero* or *compañera* who shows up?

Silence. I hesitate an instant.

"Then it's not true," says my *responsable*.

It was the moment I was waiting for. Stammering, I tell him I am willing to go.

My captain leaves.

Now comes the worst part. I have to get myself ready to go to that street and work out enough freedom of movement to run off, and have them shoot and kill me.

I even see myself running and running and they don't catch me. I know where I'd go, to the house of a friend, an older woman, the mother of a friend. I have tried to forget all telephone numbers, but hers sticks in my head. I could forget everything but not that number. And if I did forget it, I had figured out a way to bring it back. Six digits, the first, third and fifth are powers of two; the second, fourth and sixth are the same number, nine.

The hours go by, days go by, and I am not taken to the contact. I am not able to get myself shot.

28

The memory of the ear is amazing. In the winter of 1972, hundreds of prisoners go through the barracks, all tortured. A woman has been arrested and is tortured only when the officers have free time, apparently with little conviction. In the silence of a quiet night, I can hear her screams. She has a powerful voice, her screams resound in the torture room, climb the stairs, go through the walls, and explode on prisoners' eardrums. She is tortured one or two nights a week.

A relationship of mutual knowledge and dependence and even confidence develops between the prisoner and his torturer, so that a prisoner who has been in the barracks for a couple of months may make remarks about other things than what connect him to his torturer, which is information the other wants, and the prisoner does not want to give.

That woman who screams like I never knew a person could scream, and who does not appear to have much information to give, causes two or three prisoners, myself among them, to ask our respective *responsable*s why they don't let her go, as she obviously has nothing to tell, and anyway is sick in the head.

The *responsable* tells me it's not like that. He knows she has information and only pretends to be mad.

Days later the woman's screams disappear. She may have been freed or transferred, or may have died in torture. I've never seen her, don't know her name, or how old she is. But the sound of her screams remain in my head.

We called her "the mad-dog woman" and it was she, many years later, sitting opposite me at a dinner in Stockholm, whom I would recognize by her voice.

29

It must be that a torturer creates an idea of a human being only he can live up to. To inflict pain deliberately has to be a unique experience. To see a man or woman made into mincemeat, who before arrest was leading a normal life, now turned into humiliated flesh—in pain, screaming, begging, crawling—this is bound to provide a view of the human condition beyond what society permits.

It is absolutely impossible to think that at the time of torture, or after, even years later, the torturer does not reflect on his experiences. Not that he condemns himself: he may justify to himself what he's done, he may even be convinced that if necessary he would do it again. What he cannot do is fail to think about it.

Perhaps at the time of making decisions, planning arrests, planning torment, the torturer does not ask himself questions, feels no need to answer why and to what purpose. But one day he is bound to think it through, get to where there are no ideological, political, or professional excuses, nothing. One day, alone, face to face with his conscience, how will the torturer answer to himself?

30

I think every torturer develops his own skills and techniques. He learns to use common instruments— water, electricity, garrote—as one learns to use any tool, on the material, which in his case is the body of tortured prisoners.

My *responsable* has specialized in the tank. I don't think he beats me. I'm not sure, but do know he's never done it so I could tell. Maybe during the sessions he can't avoid giving me a punch or a kick now and then, although by that point I can't tell who is doing what. I am sure his thing is the tank. In fact, years later I learn that every arrest center had its own specialized method of torture.

Where I am there are no electric prods; the tank dominates. Once, as a threat, an officer said he'd bring a prod, and then I'd see what was what. That the tank was nothing compared to the prod. But the prod never appeared, so I don't know whether it is better or worse.

But now someone gets the idea of supplementing the tank with another instrument, perhaps because the tank is a lot of work, takes strength, the floor gets wet and so do the officers.

On a certain night, torture does not begin on time. The officers are below, you can hear them, but there is no torture. Have to wait to see what they are about. It is hard to sleep when you sense you are waiting.

Suddenly the door of the torture room opens, I hear voices, someone says, "I'll get him."

Two or three run up the stairs. They come into my cell, get me up, jam me against the wall, yell, change the handcuffs to the back, begin shoving me along the corridor, push me into the hole of the stairway, I trip, they yank me up.

It's all preliminary; so far nothing happens. Shoves, shouts, light punches are bearable. But one must not show indifference, that it does not hurt. Must let them see you're afraid, can't stand more, otherwise the softening up will continue, and one would rather still be strong for what really matters, the serious torture.

31

Once below, I am informed that now I'll learn what's good for me.

My captain is present, I hear him, but he is not directing the operation.

There are no questions, only shouting, commands, threats.

They order me to raise a foot, the right one.

I place it on something that seems like a runner of a ladder.

I am to raise the other foot.

As I can't see, I don't understand what they want. I am awkward, about to fall. They help me.

I should raise the other foot, as if mounting a horse.

Someone laughs, "That's not how to get on a horse, you start with the left foot."

Not only am I awkward, they don't know how to tell me to do what they want me to do. At last they get bored and lift me outright.

They set me down and I feel a sharp stick between

my legs, on the testicles, on the coccyx. I move my body to one side. It hurts less on the rump.

Then they yell for me to sit exactly in the middle. "On your tail, on your tail!"

I move and obey, but my body leans toward the other side. Someone hits me with a stick on the right thigh. It hurts. I sit up and put my bottom on the crosspiece. When I lean toward the other side they hit me on the left leg, on the tibia. I make an effort and let the bar bury itself in the middle. I stay quiet.

Without thinking, my feet seek out the lower struts, find them, take hold, and lift the body.

I get two blows at the same time on the feet, on the toes. I must be supported only by the crosspiece in the middle that's between my legs.

This is called the *caballete* [small horse]. I had not known about it. They are trying it out on me, and learning how to use it.

The body can't balance on its coccyx, it wobbles. They hold me so I won't fall. As my hands are behind, I hold on by the crosspiece between my legs; I rise up a little, the pain lessens.

They begin to move the *caballete* as if it were a wooden horse, back and forth. This hurts. I yell.

They laugh at the novelty. And yell at me to talk, to say what I have to say.

I answer with more yells.

I don't want to talk. I can see they don't know how to use the *caballete*, they are trying it out, and I want them to see that it is unbearable, that it hurts so much I could not speak if I wanted to.

I yell some more.

This yell is natural, not the lowing as when I come out of the tank. I yell because it hurts, but also because I want to stun them so they won't ask me anything.

They stop moving the *caballete*. I keep on yelling. It hurts even when the *caballete* is still.

They declare I'll be there all night, until I decide to talk.

I don't know how much time passes, ten minutes, a quarter of an hour. Silence. It is as though I were alone, but I know there is someone watching. As a test, I lean to one side and get the crosspiece out of my crotch.

Right away I hear a voice ordering me back.

I do so, but let myself lean to the other side. The shout comes, and a blow with a stick on the leg.

And so I concentrate on trying for it not to hurt. I let the crosspiece cut into me as much as my body can stand. I know it hurts, that it will hurt worse later, but right now the area is as if anesthetized. Pain anesthetizes, and now I don't feel anything. But I still have to show it hurts, that the *caballete* is worse than the tank (thought it is not), and at the same time show them that, in spite of so much pain, I have nothing to say to them. So if I have nothing to say on the *caballete*, I'll have less in the tank.

32

I don't know how much time has gone by, one hour, two. People come into the room. Someone asks, "So?"

I don't hear the answer. I suppose the officers left

one or two soldiers on guard and went off to rest and await the results of their new instrument.

I imagine the soldier shrugging his shoulders and saying, "Nothing," with his head.

I hear the voice of the barrack commander. He is a lieutenant colonel who sometimes talks and gives orders and makes speeches to the prisoners and has nervous crises in the midst of torture sessions.

According to what an officer told me a few days ago, the head officer of the quarters can't stand what is going on here, in his house, what his subordinates are doing, and he takes tranquilizers in order to endure it. Now there is an interchange of opinions.

I manage to understand that someone had suggested the *caballete*, had seen it used elsewhere where it gave good results. But people in this quarters have their specialty, the tank, and don't believe in the new instrument, or don't know how to use it.

I hear three arguments against the *caballete*. One says, "This is not good. We'd have to leave him there all night and wait for him to think of something to say."

Another adds, "So it doesn't do anything, they could hold out for weeks sitting there."

There is another, practical voice that announces that the *caballete* is breaking down, and would have to be repaired every so often.

Then the head officer speaks, the lieutenant colonel: "Take it away."

They take me off the *caballete*. Now I feel an excruciating pain, I can barely walk. They help me climb the stairs.

When I am upstairs my captain orders handcuffs placed in front.

This means that he is not convinced of the advantages of the *caballete*. Or that he didn't think it was a good idea to try it out on me. In either case, with handcuffs in front, life improves incredibly.

I arrive at my cell, they push me toward the mattress. I lie down groping and curl up. I place my hands between my legs, grab onto my testicles, search the anus, want to reach the coccyx, want heat, heat there, heat for the bones to close that have been shoved apart.

For weeks it hurts, I walk with legs spread apart. The *caballete* never reappears.

33

They've brought the meal, I am sitting on the mattress with the hood barely raised, eating. My *responsable* enters. I place the plate on the floor and stand up.

All I have is the mattress and a blanket, and a bucket of water in the corner. My *responsable* asks what the bucket is doing there. I tell him it is to clean myself with. He does not ask how I obtained this luxury. No one has a bucket of water in his cell. My captain is condescending towards me, he does not order it taken away, although he knows this is not normal.

He tells me he went by the door of my parents' house, to see where they lived, how they lived. I don't believe it was only out of curiosity, nor do I care whether he saw them or not. Although I know he will lie, I ask him how my family is.

They're fine, he can tell me no more.

He asks me about events he does not know whether or not I knew about, but needs to know, having been assigned the investigation.

He knows I'm not going to tell him even if I do know, at least not just like that, for free, without torture.

He is not interrogating me, only commenting on the work he has been assigned, as if we were friends, colleagues, or neighbors.

In passing he insinuates, warning me, that if I do know what he is asking and do not tell him, he will be offended, and then won't be able to trust me any longer.

Actually I know exactly what he is after. I'd like to know how much he knows about what he's investigating, but he gives me no more information.

I'm worried about my bucket. It took great effort to get it. One night after a session with the tank, a soldier felt sorry for me. He let me urinate, gave me a cigarette. I made the most of the occasion to ask for water in a bucket that was in the bathroom, to wash myself. He didn't seem to mind giving it to me, although he could see I was soaked and water was the least of my needs.

34

Some nights later torture grows very violent. I can hear the moans of people tortured and officers shouting. In the corridors soldiers are tense, don't speak, aren't listening to the radio. I am on my mattress, but not sleeping.

A moment of silence comes and I hear a voice on the stairs calling my pseudonym: "Bring him down."

I enter and sense that the torture room is full. Silence, the chief officer of the quarters is to speak, the lieutenant colonel of grandiloquent discourses, of nervous crises and tranquilizers.

There is something I don't know how to define in the air. I'd call it solemnity, but that's not the word.

The lieutenant colonel does not know how to begin. He stutters. Approaches me, I sense the heat of his body near mine. He can't help making a speech, a short one this time.

He says something about how they have always been up front with me. They have been tough, but honest, straight. By contrast I am a lying son of a bitch, have been lying to them all along. From now on that will stop. It's going to be terrible for me, I'll see.

I don't know what it is he knows, but I image the worst, although it could also be nonsense. After weeks of interrogations one learns that anything can happen, and what may be important to them doesn't matter to me, and sometimes the reverse.

The lieutenant colonel finishes his discourse, stammering that I am garbage because I've been fooling them, while they've acted on their word.

Having only heard and never seen him over these weeks, I don't know whether I am being fair to the lieutenant colonel, but decide he is an imbecile. And worse in this reign of garrotes, besides being an imbecile he is a coward—and will be, forever, wherever he lives, as long as he lives, the chief of the quarters, speechifier, imbecile, and coward.

The lieutenant colonel's insults don't do anything to

me, nor do anyone's. I want to get to the bottom of things quickly, learn what new they have on me.

I sense I am in the middle of a circle of officers, or a semicircle, sense the heat of their bodies, the odor of sweat and tobacco they give out.

So far I have not heard from my captain, my reference to everything, but suppose he is there because I heard him shouting when I was upstairs. Now I know he's there because he speaks.

He is beside me.

I'm to take off my shoes.

So I know what they have found out. I have no way out, they know, but just the same I'll try to put off their realizing it.

35

I squat and begin with the left foot.

My captain says I am to take my socks off, too.

I take off the left shoe and sock, then the right.

When I finish I remain on my haunches, hiding what I don't want them to see.

They order me to stand up. Then turn around.

Someone says he sees nothing strange.

Then several stoop down around me.

One tells me to lift my feet.

I obey, first the left, then the right.

"There it is."

And I feel the boot that stomps on the right foot. They start beating on me, step on me, I jump, fall, they go after me on the floor.

"There it is," means they have seen my wounds.

Seven months ago I was shot in both feet. Even so I managed to escape. I was looked after in a clandestine hospital. First the left foot became infected, then the right, and later the right again. I was operated on four times, the last a few weeks before being arrested. When they arrested me I still had the two wounds on the right foot, the entrance and the exit. They had not noticed my limp because I forced myself so it wouldn't be noticed, so they wouldn't ask. It was not hard to hide; they had never seen me walk normally, always hooded, handcuffed, shoved along.

As they had never seen me walk normally, I stopped worrying about the limp, but I did try to do something against re-infection. First I stole soap I found in the bathroom, then got the bucket of water from the soldier. Every night, at five or six in the morning, when everyone was tired and no one checked cells, I'd get up and wash my feet, pressed the wounds so they would drain.

Now they've found the hospital where I was a patient, they have the cane I used, made from a broom handle.

I don't even have to admit I was wounded, still am, they see it.

I am wounded, and my captain is offended.

36

They take me upstairs, and oddly, there is no punishment. I sit on the mattress and rub my feet. The toes are almost broken from being stomped on. But I have an immediate advantage: I don't have to hide my wounds, I can ask for medical attention.

The next day my captain comes up to see me. He is noticeably offended because I had not told him I was wounded.

He talks and talks.

I don't say a word.

Had I told him when I was arrested, he would have had me seen by a doctor.

Am I all right from the wounds?

More or less.

I note he is not interested in my answer.

He is curious about how I had managed over the weeks for the foot not to become infected.

I no longer care if he knows, and point to the water bucket.

Silence.

I fear they will take it away. Maybe better not to have told him.

Ah, was that what it was for? He kicks at the bucket.

The soap I've got hidden, wrapped in plastic under the mattress.

He goes. Returns. Seems he wants to tell me something and does not know how. Or maybe not, maybe he's impressed by the wounds, that I preferred not to say anything and suffered alone. I don't know. I can't read his face because I don't see him. When we talk I look from below the hood, I see his boots. In any case I don't want to know what is going on. I too want to tell him something, the idea that came to me last night. First I have to find out whether he is only offended or also annoyed. I am concentrating on that. I don't know where I stand with him, because it's a game. Not even a game, a small trick, but it matters to me. If I say it to him, it is to get what I want, not for him to deny me.

Now he is leaving.

I get up the nerve when he is in the corridor and call.

He comes back

What is it?

"Could you have me seen by a doctor?"

Silence. He thinks.

He'll do what he can.

Days go by and no doctor appears.

I go on washing my foot. Although I don't want them to see me, now it isn't as serious if someone does catch me doing so.

37

For several weeks they have been asking about Francisco. The seven of us in the cells know who Francisco is. Francisco is a pseudonym; I don't know whether anyone here knows what his real name is. Probably, but I don't. Nor do I know where he is just now, nor have a way of finding out. That gives me certain peace of mind: never, through me, will they find him.

This is a strange night. There is no torture. One has become used to marking the time. Don't know the hour, but have the idea by now they ought to have begun to torture. Maybe they'll start in awhile, best be prepared. Time passes and torture does not begin. This is worrisome. When it starts you hear the screaming of the tortured plus the shouts of the torturers. That is the normal situation. Even with the screaming, if you are on the mattress, you can sleep. But, silence is a premonition, something different is up, and that is not good. Here nothing different can be good.

Silence continues all night: barely a cough, or the voices of soldiers on guard listening to the radio. This may mean they have gone out on a major operation along with a lot of personnel. It may mean a great many other things that the mind invents to be doing something, find an answer. Finally I go to sleep.

Toward dawn, my *responsable* comes into the cell. He has me get up and leads me hooded down the stairs to the lower floor. Everything is very quiet. As I go down I can hear a vehicle stopping. By the easy way the captain is treating me and by the sound of the motor, I suppose I am to be transferred. But something is strange: my handcuffs are in front and not changed to the back. Transfers are never made with handcuffs in front, not even within the quarters. Are they taking me out to shoot me? It is a possibility. I don't know whether it has already occurred, if they have taken someone out there and killed him, but I've often thought that some night they'd take us and shoot us in some ditch.

Oddly, the idea does not frighten me: it isn't courage, it's insensibility. I am twenty-three years old, and it will pain my parents to lose this son. There are many things I'd like to talk with them about, those one discovers through the passage from adolescence to adulthood and never finds time to say to parents. There is my sister, who is a girl, who has a lot to learn. With her I'd like to talk a lot, accompany her as she becomes an adult. I'll die without seeing them; they will suffer for me.

That is the only thing that makes me sad.

38

When we reach the end of the staircase the captain has me walk the two meters that separate us from the door, whereupon the idling vehicle stops. By the sound of the motor I can tell it is a small vehicle, not a truck.

I sense someone open the door at the back, which convinces me it is a pickup. The captain makes me go forward and I hit my shin against the fender. I understand they want me to get in, so I raise my foot and lower my head. Then the captain lifts my hood—he does not want me to get in, but to look, and see.

Forty centimeters in front of me is the face of Francisco, sitting on the floor of the pickup, very pale, his blue-green eyes half open, a blanket over his back and arms.

I don't want the captain to see that I know who it is. I look at his eyes trying to guess something, to say I don't know him, that not only do I not know who he is, I don't know who Francisco is.

Francisco looks at me. He does not speak, nor blink, nor shut his eyes. He does not give me the sign I am waiting for. I think they have undone him in torture; he can't take any more. All this happens in seconds.

The captain asks if I know who this man is. I figure that if Francisco has not said who he is, and if he has stood it this long, I have no right to say he is who they have been looking for for weeks, at least unless they torture me. Although they'll find out anyway, I must let myself be tortured before admitting that he is Francisco.

In those seconds, with half my body in the pickup, my head has to think up an answer. I gather up a little courage and tell the captain I don't know who it is.

Then the soldier in the front seat moves and his elbow touches Francisco's shoulder. Francisco's body falls to the side and I see blood on his neck. Francisco's pallor is the pallor of death.

"It does not matter. We know who it is. And you know, too. It is Francisco."

The captain is annoyed. He places his hand at the back of my hood, squeezes it against my face and neck, makes me climb the stairs at a run. I can't breathe, trip, fall down. My captain raises me by the hood. It's as if he's choking me, I'm asphyxiated. When we get to the first floor he throws me on the floor and tells the soldiers to place me *de plantón*.

"No water or bathroom or anything for this one, until further orders. Understood?"

"Yes, my captain."

39

Later, in the cell, and even now almost thirty years later, I keep wondering at what moment did I tell the captain that I did not know who the man before me was. Did I answer before or after I knew he was dead? I would like to think I answered before I saw they had killed him. Before, not after. If I answered before, when I thought he was still alive, it would have been a way of saying, "Francisco, I'm not turning you in. At least I can promise I won't turn you in for free. It will only be in torture. Whatever happens, it will be in torture."

But I don't know at just what point I answered. I'll never know.

40

One morning they wake us up early and give us breakfast. Next they adjust hoods and throw us on the bed of an army truck, and we leave the barrack. We can see several military vehicles following. There are probably some ahead.

When I was arrested, the military thought I didn't know where I was, but from the floor of the pickup I mentally followed the streets they took me through, and knew which quarters we were in. Now, hooded on the bed of the truck, my mind again traces the route. Then I get lost and don't know where we are going. Soon the truck goes down a steep incline. When it stops and they have us get down, we are in the basement of Police Headquarters. I'd already been here on my first arrest, two years ago.

We don't know what they've brought us for. The officer in charge distributes his personnel. They take off our hoods and we go down labyrinthine corridors: one officer ahead, another behind, two soldiers to the sides, armed, tense. They try to keep the civil police from hitting us. They do well. From every office, from every door, police appear to insult us, they want to hit us, say we should be shot.

We arrive at a place I have never been before, a hall of mirrors. A very large room, one wall a mirror. Prisoners are to walk along the mirrors, with whom on the other side? Police, probably police collaborators, informers, taxi drivers, waiters in bars, owners of kiosks, hotels, rooming houses. They will remember these faces if ever we are in the street again. They could recognize us and inform. Police do it all over the world.

The parade begins. Prisoners are made to walk one at a time and the captain who has directed the transfer from the quarters gives out information, his voice loud, proud, to those who are on the other side of the mirror.

When it is my turn the officer announces, besides the usual details, "This individual is lame, from being shot in the foot."

Now I do realize I am lame. As I have not walked for months, I did not know I could not move without difficulty. I sense that I am not permanently lame but will get over this, yet over the months I'll see that no, I cannot move three toes of the right foot, which makes it hard to walk. For two years I'll spend hours exercising so as to walk straight. It does not show, but even yet when I get up on a cold morning, I am a little lame.

41

For hours they have us parading before the mirrors. Suddenly there is a pause. They put us in a dark place, which smells bad, a corridor that leads nowhere or is shut off. Soldiers who had been protecting us spread out, go off a few meters to smoke, go to the bathroom. Then four, five police get in the corridor and beat up on us. We fall to the floor. There is an uproar; it's dark, you hear the complaints of the prisoners, the insults of the police. Soldiers come to get the police out of there. Same thing repeated throughout the day, at each break. Although the soldiers are on alert, suddenly a civil policeman gets into the corridor and beats up whoever he can get his hands on.

The army officers have gone to eat. I need to urinate. I ask the soldiers. I am handcuffed behind. They look for the key to the handcuffs. The officers have taken them. I do not even dream that the sergeant left in charge would be willing to go ask for the key. I am about to wet my pants, try to hold off a little longer.

A soldier comes up and says that if I want, he will help me.

I say yes.

We walk a few meters. I am a little afraid; maybe he wants to turn me over to the police to beat me up. But I can't hold off any longer, I am going to wet myself. I take the risk.

The soldier leads me to the bathroom. We go in. It is an uncomfortable situation for me, also for him. I don't know what to say, how to behave. Nor he.

Then he sets his gun against the wall, bends toward me, opens my fly, takes out my penis.

I urinate, with pleasure, and shame, for me, for the soldier. When I finish I am in a worse state than before, fly open, penis hanging out, hands behind my back. I look

at the soldier. He laughs, nervous like a child. I laugh
too, also nervous like a child. He bends over, replaces my
penis, closes the fly. We look at each other. I am moved by
what he has done. I want to tell him so. Don't find words.

"Thank you."

"You're welcome."

I want to say something more. Don't know how.

He takes me back to my place.

42

It is October 1972, almost five months since my arrest.
One day they take me to a military court on a naval base.
The judge is not there, there is an anonymous clerk, fat,
sympathetic. He has an edict written up at the quarters.
He asks me accessory things. He does not care what I tell
him. He has me sign a paper.

In the course of ten years I'll go once a year to the
military court, sometimes twice. I am never interested
in anything they say, in what I sign. I always sign, except
once, when they state the sentence. I ask to speak with
my lawyer. He is a colonel, lawyer by trade, whom I have
never seen.

They said the lawyer called to say he could not come.

"Then I don't sign."

A colonel says that does not matter. They will sign.
That will do.

They put the handcuffs on behind me, take me to the
door, give me a hard push. When I am about to hit my
head hard against the wall, two prisoners sitting down
and handcuffed at their backs, stand up and place their

bodies in front of me. I fall on top of them with all my weight. Tenderness of prisoners, to keep another from splitting his head open.

In subsequent trips to the court I would grow to know—almost all of us would know him—a young, blonde gentleman, lawyer or law student, not military, or maybe assimilated, but not military by training. He's one of the "civilians" in this civil-military dictatorship. Sympathetic, he has a fountain pen he hands prisoners for signing. The pen only works at a certain angle. The little blonde always says the same thing, "Hold it like this, please, because it has a *yeito*."

Like that, in Portuñol, "It has a *yeito*."*

As I write, twenty-eight years have passed since that first time I went to the court. Inexplicably, I still feel for that well-combed, well-dressed little blonde angel the same contempt I felt then. I don't feel hatred, not for him nor for the torturers: I feel contempt.

During the first days in the barracks I kept track of the date. Then I lost count. Now, on my first trip to the court, at the moment of signing, I learn it is October 24. Today is my parents' birthday, the two on the same day. My mother is forty-two, my father forty-eight.

---

*Meaning that there is a knack or trick to using the pen. Portuñol is a useful street combination of Spanish and Portuguese spoken along the borders of all the countries surrounding Brazil. Brazilians tend to be more conversant in Spanish than the other way around; in Uruguay, Portuguese is not regularly taught in the schools. Some education administrators (and others) in Uruguay disapprove so strongly of Portuñol that they have suggested barring television programs from Brazil, the source of popular soap operas.

43

Now, after having my hearing in court, I have hopes they will not go back to torturing me. There is the belief that after a court appearance, a prisoner has rights, the rights of the prosecuted.

In a few days I am transferred to a cell on the sixth floor of Police Headquarters. There is a cot, no mattress, the window is blocked. The cell is so small I can't walk or even stand up, only sit or lie on the cot. No matter, this is a luxury hotel compared to the solitary cell in the barrack.

Little by little I get an idea about the place. There are hundreds of prisoners in Police Headquarters, the fourth floor is for women, some pregnant, very young. The third is called *La pelada* [slang for "empty," the bare one] because it has no light or water. In compensation, they say, the cells are open, prisoners can move about the whole floor.

I begin to organize myself, establish contact with other prisoners. The second day I hear someone say my name at the grate leading to the floor. The cell door opens.

I am to go out.

They take me to an office. There is an army captain. Tall, looking offended. He puts handcuffs on me behind, and throws me against a chair. He begins asking me all sorts of things, none having to do with me.

He says I have no time to lose, if I don't answer right away he will take me to his barrack, in another city.

He can assure me that I'll soon be crawling along the floor and kissing his boots.

That he'll make me wish I'd never been born.

That what they've done with me so far is nothing, I am still in one piece, as if untouched.

If he gets hold of me, there will be nothing left.

He insults me every way possible. He is crude, and wants to appear crude.

At first I can't respond to what he is asking, although I might have some side information. I know he is only trying to scare me, but, although I know it, I can't help being scared. I realize this beast is capable of carrying through with his promises.

He tells me that a man in his barrack, whom I know, has been reduced to a little animal.

"He walks on four legs, like a little animal. That's how you'll end up."

I try to make him see I don't know what he's talking about, and at the same time, not let him think I am lying. I don't want to go back to torture. I have to be realistic.

The conversation, if that's what it can be called, continues. I note he gets bored, that maybe he's had to come to Police Headquarters to see if he can fish out something.

Someone comes in to speak to him.

The captain loses interest in me. He leaves the room. In a while he comes back. He removes my handcuffs.

"Take him away."

As I leave, he yells, "This evening, you're going with me."

I keep thinking about that all day. It is not torture, only the threat of torture, but just the same does not leave my head quiet for an instant. Had he said it only to frighten me? Will he come get me?

Late at night I relax. At least today they won't take me.

44

A week has gone by. It is late. Without preamble, they have me leave the cell, "With everything."

That means with a plastic bag where I have toothbrush and tooth paste, soap, a towel, a book by Ray Bradbury I got hold of.

"Where am I going? Another cell?"

Nothing, not a word.

I see I am not being taken to another cell. We go down in the elevator to the ground floor. There is a jeep. They hood me, and handcuff me behind. We go back to the beginning.

I am in another barrack. They put me in a boxcar. As the army does not have room for so many prisoners, it has decommissioned boxcars and uses them as prison cells. There is a chair. They let me sit down.

I mentally go through what they might ask me. I tell myself it can be nothing serious. But you never know. They can torture a lot for stupid things. Anyway, it won't be serious. Relax.

I realize I am a "veteran." I've been in prison for months. I am healthy, clean, my head works. My youth endures a lot.

An hour later I sense someone come into the car. More than one, I can't tell how many. Under the hood I see the boots. They are officers. Soldiers don't have those kinds of boots. And they are cavalry officers. This change does not matter. Or does it?

Those who enter are joking, say my last name, my nickname. A hand raises my hood a few centimeters, enough to expose my cheek. It places the butt of a revolver against my cheek. It does not scare me, but it pushes against the revolver and the point against the bone hurts.

"Do we kill him?" says one, not the one who shoves the gun.

"No, better later," says another voice.

Now I realize there are three.

One asks if I know where I am.

I am going to provoke them. Without much trouble I can test them out, see what sort they are.

"I don't know where I am. But I know it is a cavalry quarters."

How do I know?

By the boots.

The one with the gun asks if I know who he is.

I say yes.

The rest laugh.

"He recognizes you?"

He lowers his gun.

"What's my name?"

"I don't remember your name, but I know what they call you."

More laughter.

"What do they call me?"

I tell him the nickname.

He was a classmate in high school, eight years ago. I had not seen him since. The memory of the ear amazes me, to have remembered the voice of this individual for so long.

Laughter fills the car. They leave.

45

It's night. They've fed me. No mattress has appeared. Maybe I'm supposed to sleep sitting up. But it is still early, better wait. Haven't seen any other prisoner, don't have an idea of the space. The boxcar is in an open space, I hear voices of soldiers who pass by, footsteps on the gravel.

I don't know where they torture. My head tries to organize the space, keep track of time, pick up clues. I sense it is important to know where they torture, and don't know why, as one place is the same as another.

When they take me to the bathroom I can't tell anything. Barracks latrine, no characteristics that will help locate me.

I'm lost; my thoughts go without my being able to stop them: three hours, four, footsteps on the gravel. They are coming this way.

"Bring him down!"

The soldiers have me go down the steps of the boxcar. Here we go, now things will start.

We go into a strange place. The first thing that happens is they bang my head against something. Someone gives me a clue where we are, "Careful with the stick."

That detail, I don't know why, tells me we are in a country store.

The hitting starts, casual blows. Nothing serious. "Now, you're going to see what's good for you, Liscano."

Someone hits me in the face. It hurts, but more than hurting it bothers me. Only once did they hit me in the face, with a fist, in the first barrack. It doesn't do anything, hitting the face. I mean, it does not bring any result, but is very annoying, and can leave marks. It's preferable, for example, to the rubber hose on arms or legs, which is very painful and leaves no marks. I don't know why, but I prefer a good blow on the back or chest than a punch in the face.

I realize they are happy. Or not happy but entertained. I learn they have a woman prisoner who was a girlfriend of mine a couple of years ago.

I tell them I didn't know. Not even why they arrested her.

They tell me she has other opinions.

"Impossible."

"We'll see."

They have nothing to ask. That's what my head says. But be careful. They can torture me even with nothing to ask.

They have me sit down. They raise the hood. They don't care if I see them.

That makes me try another style, cheeky, a torture "veteran." I ask for a cigarette.

They tell me they'll give me one if I cooperate.

I don't care. Give me a cigarette and we'll talk. But I know nothing that can interest them.

The one in front of me, a first lieutenant, lights a cigarette and places it between my lips.

I ask them to change the handcuffs to the front.

They laugh, think I am showing off, abusing their "hospitality."

They change the handcuffs as I asked.

They shout, interrupt. I realize they are not interested in asking me anything. They talk nonsense.

Suddenly they find what to ask.

Did I go to bed with the woman they have imprisoned?

They ask in the grossest manner.

I don't answer.

They insist.

"Was she a virgin when you knew her? What can she do in bed?"

This bothers me a lot. It's irrational to be bothered, it should not matter to me, but I can't help it.

I don't answer.

They go on.

"How does she do it? How does she do it?"

I realize silence is not a sufficient answer. So it will be clear to them what I think, word for word, I tell them, in a low voice, very sharply, "To that I am not answering anything."

What I want to tell them with my tone of voice is that a man does not tell nor ask such things. And with what is left of me, even in these conditions, for that reason I continue to be *un macho*.

Silence.

Maybe I made a mistake and they don't understand and this is going to turn out to be very difficult. I am going to have to do something else, and don't want to. I don't want to talk to these guys, don't want to be beaten.

But yes, they do understand and change the subject.

At any rate, for refusing to answer I lose the cigarette. The one who takes it away does it roughly and takes with it part of the skin off my lip. It hurts, and bleeds.

"Well, it's over," says the first lieutenant.

"Yes, we're not getting fucked around any more," says the one from my high school.

Now they'll begin to torture, I tell myself.

They have me stand up.

"Take him to the stables," says the lieutenant to a soldier.

I guess that for now they will not torture me.

They put on the hood. Along the way I realize we are not going back to the boxcar. That the officer had said "stables."

I tell the soldiers who are taking me that I want to get my bag in the boxcar.

They hesitate. Say no. The order was "to the stables."

46

We go into a place that actually is a stable. From under the hood I see hay bales. Horse feed. They throw me onto a mattress. I think about my bag in the boxcar, I've lost it. I'll have a lot of rowing to do to get it back.

From the mattress I begin to see: a hay bale, mattress, hay bale, mattress, and on each mattress a man or woman. Little by little someone moves, speaks, asks for something, is taken to be tortured, returns soaked. I see there are more men than women.

After awhile they throw the plastic bag at me with my things, it hits me on the head.

The days pass. They don't torture me, don't interrogate. I organize my life on the mattress. See familiar faces. Begin to see women. They are hooded, but you can tell the body beneath the hood, hear the voices. It is a pleasure to see them, even here, even in these conditions, although they are a wreck. There is another odor in the air, odor of female that mixes with ours, with the stables.

Have been here a week, without moving from the mattress.

One afternoon a sergeant comes.

Get my things ready. That is, the plastic bag.

We leave. They've brought me for nothing. I don't know the date, nor just then that it's my last passage through the barracks, the last time they will put a hood on me, that I'll have gone past a torture room.

Sit and Wait for What Comes

1

I don't know why they take off my hood and handcuffs before having me get into the jeep. Perhaps some rule having to do with the ordering of equipment, or an odd command about transferring prisoners. I give the matter a moment's thought, but can't figure it out.

A soldier removes his necktie and ties my thumbs together, and then my wrists. This I have not seen before, ingenious, as good as handcuffs. Impossible to do anything with thumbs tied together. I am intrigued by this new information. So I won't be able to see, they put a blind over my eyes.

I ride sitting down, backwards to the motion of the jeep. In front are the driver and a sergeant, a soldier on each side of me. I see I have descended noticeably in rank: earlier, I'd always been guarded by my *responsable* and two officers. Now the transfer is in the hands of a sergeant. I am glad. It is better not to be "important," to pass unnoticed. I never was "important," but was thought so.

In the jeep, no one speaks. By wriggling my brows I manage to shift the blinds. I see where we are, recognize the street. I begin to think about jumping off the jeep, not to get myself killed but to escape. If I jumped from the moving jeep I could fall on my back, hit my neck. I'd have to turn over in the air so as not to fall on the cement. The soldiers are armed with loaded M2s, automatics, probably without a clip. While I got my balance and started to run they'd have time to shoot. It is day. The possibility that they wouldn't hit me is slim. And if they didn't hit me, where would I go? I have nowhere to go, I don't know who has not been arrested. While I think up this useless escape plan, we reach headquarters. Now I won't try it.

Later, for years, dreaming awake about impossible flights, I will remember this chance as the only one I had to escape. I'll tell myself that if I had done it I might have saved myself, the soldiers might have delayed in shooting, I would have run and they'd never have found me. I also might have died that morning. Maybe better dead than a prisoner? No. But the images keep coming back every few months, the prisoner's dream: flee, run, run through an immense white empty space, without bars, without limits. At the far end a light like dawn or sunset. I never know whether the sun is setting or rising. I run and run. Soon I begin to walk, to search. There are no roads, I can go in any direction, follow my feet, walk, walk indefinitely. This is liberty, the liberty of dreams, the possibility of deciding, choosing, doing, not doing, stop doing.

For years and forever, liberty is running through an immense white open space in the half light.

2

Back from cavalry barracks to Police Headquarters in Montevideo. In a few days a major event: they transfer me to a cell where there are other prisoners. A space four by three meters. We are fourteen. We are "in storage"—in the Central Prison, but only in storage. This makes us laugh, as if we were merchandise.

The lack of space does not bother me. It is the first time in six months I can talk to someone who is not my *responsable*. I begin to catch up with what has been happening in the country and in barracks where I have not been. There are books, although it is hard to find an isolated corner to concentrate to read. At night talk goes on until late. There are not enough mattresses for everyone because there isn't room on the floor. We sleep as we can, but it is infinitely better than the solitary cells. It is not cold, people tell stories, make jokes. That's the good part, not the comfort but the companionship.

In a few days I realize that being shut up with so many people makes for tension, small rivalries.

One afternoon they bring in a man who has been isolated for months. We offer him food, reading matter, whatever he wants.

Nothing, he's not interested in anything but conversing.

It begins to darken and two or three start beating on a drum, on some plastic buckets, on a box. The newcomer gets up, tries out a few dance steps.

Shouts, applause.

He goes on dancing another instant.

And then he keeps on, does not stop. He moves, his body seeks the rhythm, finds it.

Room is made for him in the center of the cell, little by little a chorus of men forms sitting on the floor, on the mattresses, around the one who is dancing.

And the newcomer dances and dances. With his eyes closed he turns, lifts his arms, moves his hips, shoulders, bends his body, holds, turns in the other direction.

The musicians get bored, they tire, but the music can't stop, others pick up the drum, the abandoned plastic bucket. The music must go on so this man can keep flying, traveling in his dancing, in his felicity. He's happy, happy, you see it in his face, in his closed eyes, in his hands, in the freed body. He's been alone for months when his body has not felt the heat of a friendly body near. And he dances, his body dances an hour, an hour and a half?

Is he sick?

In any case, sick and happy.

When at last he stops, he smiles, looks at us. He starts to speak.

Is there anything to eat?

He is somebody else, he's forgotten that he held us enthralled for over two hours, happy, worried. He's visited the spot he needed to visit, who knows where or with whom. Now he is someone else, and he's here. He wants to eat.

3

One day there is a party. One of the men in the cells
learns that his wife, a prisoner in another location, has
given birth to a baby girl. Mother and daughter are well.
The father's eyes fill with tears. We embrace him, sing to
him, joke.

Then the father, resolutely, does something no one
can believe. He gets a needle and thread, takes off his shirt
and begins cutting it up in little pieces, and sewing the
pieces together. Then he gets a marker. He has wonderful
skill in his hands. In half an hour he has made a doll,
two big eyes, long eyelashes, red lips. It is his present for
his newborn daughter. The doll is beautiful. It is the first
time, and still the only time, that I see the "birth" of a doll:
a singular doll, born of a man's hands, among men.

4

Two weeks later I am transferred again. This time
to Punta de Rieles, a building in the middle of the
countryside although near the city, once a Catholic
nunnery.

After a week, another transfer. One early morning
they call me, take me to what has been the chapel. There is
a group of some fifteen prisoners.

Where are they taking us?

Someone has found out we are going to *Libertad*
Prison. We have heard a lot of talk about the place, but
only rumors. No one knows what it's like, what to expect.

They put us in a truck entirely enclosed, what we call
a *ropero* [clothes closet]. They handcuff us in an incredible

manner. Sitting in a circle on the floor facing inward, my right hand is handcuffed to the left hand of the man to my left, or the hand of the other that is farthest from me, and my left hand with the right hand of the man on my right, and so on around the circle.

We travel for more than an hour. The prison is some fifty kilometers from Montevideo. When we arrive there begins a great uproar. They take off the handcuffs and throw us off the truck, with the bags. When I fall, a soldier with a garrote gets me up, twists my arm at the shoulder and starts to run behind me, making me run, with the bag. We go up a staircase. We run upstairs for several floors, I don't know how many. I can't breathe. The soldier tires too, but keeps on pushing me.

At last we walk up the stairs. I see a long line of metal doors painted gray. There is a soldier next to an open door. When we get there the other pushes me into the cell and the door slams behind me, then the click of the lock.

It is early morning.

I look out the window. There is a wire fence, lights. We are in the country but I don't see it. I do make out the horizon. I try to orient myself. If that is the horizon, then is that the Río de la Plata?

I think so.

Once oriented, I lie down and sleep.

5

The slamming of the little window on the cell door wakes me. Breakfast. I barely have time to eat when I am taken out running. This time it's running downstairs, more difficult. They put me in a place with showers. Shouting, they tell me to take off my clothes and shower. I have no towel. I dry myself with the clothes. Next they give me a gray uniform and a pair of *alpargatas* [shoes with rope soles and canvas tops]. I get dressed and shod. They have me sit on a box and a soldier shaves my head. They take me a few meters away to a door.

It is the infirmary. Men dressed in white, with green uniforms underneath, and military boots. They take down information.

"Are you diabetic, have you had tuberculosis, heart problems, syphilis?"

"Now take off your clothes."

They look me over. They don't see the wounds in the feet. I try not to let them.

"Turn around."

"Lean over."

"Spread apart your buttocks."

I don't know what they want. I don't move.

He puts his finger on my shoulder.

"You hear?"

I say I do not understand.

Ironic: "Grab your buttocks with your hands and open up. Understand?"

I understand. There go the buttocks.

"Next!"

I go out and am taken to the same cell where I was. After awhile they have me pick up my bag that is in the large corridor. It is comforting to be reunited with the bag, like the prisoner's house where he has all he needs, all he is allowed to have, that is authorized.

In the cell they have placed a mattress, a pillow, two sheets, two blankets, a pillowcase, a deep dish, a shallow dish, a dessert plate, an aluminum jug. Everything smells of disinfectant.

When I finish looking over all these new things they have left me, and am still trying to "see" myself in the hard gray uniform with a number on the chest, and I realize I am cold because I have nothing on under the uniform, the door opens.

Outside are a sergeant and two soldiers.

I am to gather up my things, everything, mattress too.

Now I have a lot of stuff. It is hard to gather it all up at once. I do what I can. I wrap the mattress in a sheet, put the objects inside, and carry the load on my shoulders. I leave a hand free for the bag. We go down the stairs. It's awkward, but over the years I will get practiced in carrying "everything" at once.

We reach another floor. I don't know which. They put me in cell number fourteen. I look out the window for awhile, countryside without a tree. That on the horizon must be the Río de la Plata or the Río Santa Lucía.

I make the bed, reorganize my things. I sit to wait. I don't know for what, but you have to wait for something. After a long while I know: I am sitting down to wait for the armored truck of fools, that one day will take me on the absurd journey to liberty.

6

I am on the second floor of the Establecimiento de Reclusión No 1, known as *Libertad* Prison. I am twenty-three years old and prisoner number 490. It is, I think, November 23, 1972. I limp on my right foot. In this place and on this floor I will live twelve years, four months, and twenty days.

Here I will become an adult male, grow my first gray hairs, make my best friends, read hundreds of good, bad, and mediocre books. I will learn a great deal about other prisoners, and about myself. I'll suffer cold, punishments, illnesses, discomforts, worries, depressions. I'll live through new miseries, large and small, of mine and of others. I'll witness amazing acts of loyalty, tenderness, and affection by men who are the same as I, deprived of everything. I shall feel the beginning of aging. I will decide to become a writer.

When I leave the second floor, I will be as lame as at the beginning, again on the right foot, because of a sprain playing the last football match that political prisoners will have played in that prison. On March 13, 1985, they will take me to Police Headquarters in Montevideo and there I will spend a night on the fourth floor, stretched out on a mattress because I can't walk. When the armored truck leaves me at my parents' house, they will not be there. My sister will await me. We'll weep together a moment. That night I'll go to bed very late.

The next day I'll get up at half-past five in the morning, obsessed with doing "something" with my liberty. I won't know what to do with my life, except one thing, making a clean copy of my papers from prison:

La mansión del tirano, El informante, the diary of *El informante*, my poems, my notes. And I will dedicate myself to writing. I don't know whether for the rest of my life, but at least until the day I have nothing more to say. Writing, until further notice, will be the center of my life.

That morning I feel life belongs to me, it is mine, mine alone, and I can do with it what I want. I know that is a lot more difficult than being in prison.

March 15, my first hours as a free man. Three days later, March 18, 1985, I'll be thirty-five years old. At thirty-six there still is a lot one can do. In spite of time spent in prison, my body continues strong and healthy. How many years do I have left? And how many more would I want to live? Thirty? Not so many. Let's say twenty. In those twenty years I should live my liberty, never make a mistake, or as few as possible. At the time I think I am capable of achieving that, setting a goal and heading for it, against whatever gets in the way, without mistakes.

I don't realize at the time that for years that will be my way of living, hardly wanting to, or knowing or believing that I am driven by an urgent passion to take advantage of the time, to do, learn, know—typical prisoner behavior. Many things remain outside my interests, and when I realize it, it is late again, but it was my choice. That choice, electing certain interests rather than others, even if mistaken, was how I exercised my liberty.

Some nights, among friends, I'll tell amusing prison stories, but for a long time refuse to write about prison, as I feel incapable of telling, in writing, more than interminable anecdotes of humiliations, that lacked complexity or literary form.

It took twenty-seven years before I could find a voice that could speak of old times. One day the voice understood that the relationship between an isolated individual and the word has enough meaning and literary interest to be told, so I wrote, "The Language of Solitude," and thought that was all I was capable of saying.

But another day, a year later, suddenly the voice opened up, took over, wanted to speak, to tell, with or without a proper order, with or without literary quality. And the voice wouldn't stop, told me to write, to recover events, sensations, feelings that I did not remember.

I was fifty-one at the time, a more mature man, which is a polite way of saying I was growing old. I was just as disoriented before the exercise of liberty as on March 14, 1985, when I rode in the truck of fools. I am still looking, trying out, thinking at times I have found it, others that I have lost it. On occasional sad days, at dismal hours, I think the years in prison robbed me of opportunities—to study, for example. But never, not for a moment, do I feel prison impoverished me spiritually.

Thus, one night in 1999, twenty-seven years after being taken prisoner, I wrote:

Before our thirties, either in power, or dead.
We were young, a lot of us, and
    had come into life only
    to change the world.

Life went on, and nothing was as we had said.
   It was prison, torture, thousands
   dead.
Even so, when we meet, the
   memory of the dream of boyhood
   still fills the heart, that once cared enough
   to believe so much.
So I think that had there been another possibility
   for me I would not have wanted it.
Because, and forgive me for saying so, I owe
   to that dream the joy of having
   known some of the best of men.

7

The body, that for so many years was all I had, in spite
of beatings, miseries, the disgust I once felt for it, now
on the road to old age, friendly animal, stays loyal to me.
   I'd like to say, and do say to it, with the most
ordinary words that a man in the habit of working
with words can find: I would like to be able to chose
the death of my body, the day, the place, and the means.
That it be serene and placid. And something else
absolutely irrational: I'd like my bones to be joined with
those of my parents, if that is possible. All I ever asked
of my body in torture was that it allow me one day to
look them in the face with dignity.

Afterword

> In November 1972 a prison for political prisoners was
> inaugurated in Uruguay, a strange prison, a sort of
> kingdom of contrary logic, where the word was central,
> but by its absence and distortion. It was a place where
> words lost their meanings more or less accepted by habit
> and by dictionaries, and acquired other, unexpected ones,
> beginning with the name of the place: *Libertad* Prison.
> —Carlos Liscano, "A Life Without Object(s)"

Liscano goes on to explain that the name of the prison, *Libertad*, came from its proximity to the town of Libertad. "Libertad" means "liberty" in Spanish, and one could be excused for thinking that the Uruguayan military meant to be cruelly ironic with the name. The simple fact is that few remember that the name of the prison is tied to its geographic locale and not to grim unintentional humor whereby the military mentality might conceive of imprisonment as a form of ideological liberation or that imprisonment would prepare the individual for the return to a "free" society that was nothing more than an exercise in state terrorism.

Although there have been a number of documentaries about prison experiences in the Southern Cone—Argentina, Brazil, Chile, and Uruguay—during the period of the neofascist tyrannies (the most famous one being Jacobo Timerman's 1981 *Prisoner Without a Name, Cell Without a Number*), none has involved such a detailed examination of the dynamics of torture as does Liscano's *Truck of Fools*. Liscano tells his own story, and it is iconic in nature, since it could be the story of any one of well over a hundred thousand prisoners in these countries between the mid-1960s and the early 1990s. It is a story of arrest, disappearance into a system that officially did not exist, interrogation through torture, confinement, and, often the disappearance by death, all without any public explanation being given beyond the fact that the nation was engaged in a "war against subversive terrorism" and that extreme measures were required by "national security."

Liscano's personal story is brilliantly told, if "brilliant" is the proper adjective for a narrative that is so marked by the systematic attempt to destroy the individual through unchecked psychological and physical assault. While there are direct references to the material experiences of torture, such as one finds in a number of official and semi-official reports on the prisons of the period and the international assessment of organizations like Amnesty International, what makes this unusually interesting is the discussion of the psychological dimension from the tortured's point of view and an attempt to evaluate the psychological experience of the torturer.

Liscano's account is a testimony to the fact that this one individual was not, ultimately, destroyed psychologically or physically. The essay "A Life Without Object(s)," from which I have taken the epigraph above, explains objectively the functioning of the *Libertad* Prison and the governing ideology on which it is grounded. However, *Truck of Fools* is a counterpoint to that objective description because it is an intensely personal narrative; moreover, it is a counterpoint to the combination of the distortion of language and the denial of human speech through which prison life functioned. By telling his own story, Liscano refutes and repudiates the language of *Libertad*, and if the importance of this document is to inform us of the existence of such a system, it allows Liscano to confirm definitively the recovery of his own personal voice despite having passed through that system.

Military regimes and political prisoners constitute a vast area of contemporary Latin American social experience, and it is important to make the appropriate differentiations among the four principal countries that experienced neofascist repression: Argentina, Brazil, Chile, and Uruguay. Although there were commonalities—clearly, the imprisonment, torture, and disappearance of dissidents—there were significant historical and sociological differences driving the circumstances of the different countries. For example, Argentina placed great emphasis on sexual issues, with the persecution of lesbians and gays being an integral part of the so-called Dirty War. By contrast, the process in Chile did not concern itself mostly with sexual issues. Although many people were killed in Brazil and Uruguay, the systematic elimination of prisoners that took place in Argentina and Chile was not an immediate policy. Antisemitism was a crucial issue in Argentina (hence the importance of Jacobo Timerman's book), but not in the other three countries (although one of the most famous guerrillas in Brazil, Iara, was Jewish). Thus, there is not a single narrative to be told, but rather a mosaic of stories that reflect the way in which, although from one point of view the matter of political prisoners is a straightforward one, from another point of view the dynamics of the respective dictatorships were very different from one country to another. This belies the U.S. or European view that the neofascist period in the mid-twentieth century in Latin America was a single, unitary phenomenon.

Liscano's narrative can, therefore, help the foreign reader understand the particular texture of the experiences of the political prisoner in Uruguay, which will not necessarily correspond in detail (although it will in general sociohistoric terms) with that of the other Southern Cone countries. More importantly, *Truck of Fools* both demonstrates the tenacity of the human spirit—such that it can experience living hell and then go on to write a brilliantly nuanced narrative—and shows how the experience of neofascism in Latin America has created its own unique cultural production, one that is not ancillary to literature of the highest order, but integral to it.

—*David William Foster*